Careers Across the Curriculum
A text for the integration of Careers Educat...
for senior educational staff, and for
use in in-service training

Careers Across the Curriculum

A text for the integration of Careers Education, for senior educational staff, and for use in in-service training

Catherine Avent O.B.E.,
Lately Senior Inspector of Careers Guidance, ILEA

Macmillan Education
London and Basingstoke

First published 1988

Published by
MACMILLAN EDUCATION LTD
Houndmills, Basingstoke, Hampshire RG21 2XS
and London
Companies and representatives
throughout the world

Printed in Hong Kong

ISBN 0-333-45233-X

Contents

PART II PRACTICALITIES

Preface

Significant vocational strands in the education of boys and girls from the age of fourteen have resulted from the Technical and Vocational Education Initiative, the Joint Board of City and Guilds of London Institute and the Business and Technician Education Council for pre-vocational education and the thrust of Industry Matters following Industry Year 1986. Attention has been sharply focused on this area of the secondary-school curriculum, while a trend down the age range into the primary schools is simultaneously advocated.

Under Grant-related In-Service Training (GRIST), school–industry links and careers education are priority areas attracting a 70 per cent grant. Headteachers therefore, can hope for resources with which to implement decisions they may be making on in-service courses for members of staff unfamiliar with the new concepts and methods of work-related education. This in no way implies that schools are 'teaching a trade' or narrowing pupils' educational experiences in the interests of employers. Far from it; the new schemes are enlarging the areas of learning available to young people.

These initiatives clearly highlight the need for schools to review their provision for careers education. The 1987 Annual Careers Conference was the occasion for an appeal from the Secretaries of State for Employment and Education to encourage Local Education Authorities to plan action to improve cooperation between careers officers and teachers. This could be achieved by systematic monitoring of their work and reinforcing the role of both professions in helping to develop in young people positive attitudes towards work, to combat sex and racial stereotyping and to recognise the influence of parents, along with their need for information on the changing pattern of employment. The publication of *Working Together for A Better Future – Careers Education and Guidance* (1987), in stressing the need for cooperation between careers advisers and representatives of the working world, presupposes provision for in-service training of teachers.

Since then the proposals for a National Curriculum appear contradictory in that the Foundation subjects do not include Careers; it will have to be included in the remaining 20–25 per cent of time or through 'themes . . . taught through other subjects'. Nor does the proposed curriculum allow much time for specific vocational subjects or such extra-mural activities as work experience. Yet the Statistical Bulletin issued by the Department of Education and Science in October 1987 shows that careers education features in the curriculum of 32 per cent of English third-year pupils, 66 per cent in fourth forms and 65 per cent in fifth forms. There is ample scope for careers education outside the Foundation curriculum or by cross-curricular arrangements.

This book has been written for secondary-school headteachers, their deputies and senior staff, as well as administrators and inspectors/advisers in LEAs who may be discussing ways of implementing policies on the in-service training of teachers for greater emphasis upon the working world. Equally it will concern lecturers in colleges and institutes of education who are preparing students for initial teaching qualifications and those running in-service courses and conferences. Implicit throughout the book is the thesis that all secondary-school teachers are concerned with the preparation of pupils for adult and working life by helping them to acquire social and life skills and to achieve a measure of employability according to their abilities and aptitudes. Each of the three parts of the book ends with suggested topics for use in staffroom discussions and school-based in-service training as well as more formal courses and study-conferences.

This is not a study of the philosophy of careers guidance or its history, or a critique of the work of the Careers Service; other authors have covered this ground. Nor is this book intended primarily for the careers advisers themselves for whom I wrote *Practical Approaches to Careers Education*. It will interest careers officers and careers teachers as they compete for resources for their work and they may have to defend its place in the school during staff meetings and committees.

During seventeen years in the Inspectorate of the Inner London Education Authority I was privileged to see many different systems for implementing policies on careers work in the curriculum. The headteachers, senior staff and careers teachers with whom I discussed their situations and problems gave me far more ideas than I could have generated myself. I am grateful to them all for much kindness and stimulation and for putting up with my enthusiasms and eccentricities. To the ILEA I owe the opportunity of a sabbatical term which enabled me to visit schools outside London to collect material and see careers education in non-metropolitan settings. I am especially grateful to headteachers John Swallow, James Dunkley, George Walker, Michael Smith, David Kenningham and M.D. Outlaw for allowing me to have extended discussions with their staffs; to Geoffrey Shaw and Roy Hollis among careers teachers, and to those attending the in-service courses led by Peter March, Ted Fooks and Phil Nodder at Bristol University School of Education and to Maurice Graham's post-graduate diploma students at the Roehampton Institute of Higher Education. In addition I have acquired ideas from conferences in different parts of the country and from the reports of working parties which several LEAs have set up to enable headteachers, careers teachers and careers officers to establish guidelines for practice in their areas.

Among the careers specialists I must acknowledge the seminal influence of Tony Watts and Bill Law of the National Institute of Careers Education and Counselling and of Beryl Fawcett whose work with the Schools Council has given her an unrivalled opportunity to see careers education in operation. They have shared their thoughts with me with unstinted generosity as have a succession of advisory teachers in ILEA who worked with me for a year at a time on secondment from their schools or colleges. My debt to my three Inspectorate colleagues, Alan Hunwicks, David Chambers and Anne Taylor cannot be measured; their enthusiasm, professionalism and friendship made my job so much more enjoyable and worthwhile. I owe a special debt to Michael Marland who first suggested this book and provided much stimulus and inspiration during our discussions of the wider context in which careers education is undertaken. Lastly, I must thank the officers and members of the National Association of Careers and Guidance Teachers for welcoming me to their meetings and conferences and for electing me, an inspector, to honorary membership.

Needless to say, none of these persons, nor the ILEA, is responsible for any of the views expressed in this book.

Catherine Avent

PART I
PREMISES AND BACKGROUND

Chapter 1
Introduction

Secondary education has become increasingly vocational in recent years and there appears to have been a greater emphasis upon the importance of public examinations as evidence of school leavers' attainments. Educational historians point out that the curriculum has veered towards and away from the supposed requirements of industry and commerce at different times during the past hundred years. They describe a crudely utilitarian programme for most pupils which was designed to produce workers for the expanding industries of the nineteenth century, while public schools emphasised instead the value of education in the humanities as preparation for a career in one of the learned professions or a leadership role in public life at home or in the empire. The growth of secondary technical schools and then their disappearance after comprehensive reorganisation has a parallel in the development of mechanics' institutes into technical colleges and later transformation into polytechnics or technological universities.

Detractors of English education accuse the schools of an anti-industrial bias which they claim is responsible for the poor performance of the national economy. Teachers are understandably resentful when their efforts are derided by employers whose expectations of school leavers may be unrealistic or inexplicit. One thing is clear, however – parents expect their children to be educated for adult life in which earning a living plays a large part. Many teachers expressed surprise when this was so clearly demonstrated in the Schools Council Enquiry No.1 *Young School Leavers* in 1968.

Recent initiatives

Official strategies to encourage more academically able youngsters to study mathematics, computer science, engineering and technology to degree and equivalent level may seem somewhat philistine to teachers steeped in the old educational tradition whereby an education in classics or philosophy, whose content had no relevance to the working world, appeared to be most highly valued. But the switch has gathered momentum inexorably and includes special scholarships for engineering students, resources being diverted from arts and humanities to science and technology, replacing the Certificate of Extended Education (CEE) by the Certificate of Prevocational Education (CPVE) and the rapid growth of the Technical and Vocational Education Initiative (TVEI).

This last change has had enormous impact since the Manpower Services Commission with its enviable financial resources has injected into secondary schools the wherewithal for a more vocationally relevant and technically biased element in the curriculum of boys and girls aged fourteen to eighteen. At the same time the Joint Board of the City and Guilds of London Institute (CGLI) and Business and Technician Education Council (BTEC) has projected its activities for students of sixteen-plus down the age range, offering incentives for pupils to undertake courses as a foundation for prevocational studies from the age of fourteen. TVEI coordinators have been appointed on individual school staffs or in areas covering several schools, and extensive programmes of in-service training have been set up to enable teachers to take part in the new curricular offerings. The technical element may be produced by extended hands-on experience of using computers so that all pupils can leave school with a basic knowledge of information technology on which specific vocational training can be based in employment or a college of further education. Other areas of exciting curriculum development include, for example, economic literacy, understanding of graphics and competence in the interpretation of charts and plans, an insight into the possibilities of robotics to replace human effort for routine mechanical operations and appreciation of the significance of design in industrial processes, buildings and products.

More significant in its long-term impact on teaching styles may be the increase in experiential learning and contacts with the outside world. No longer are teenagers confined within the school walls, but increasingly are taking part in schemes of work experience and shadowing, projects and other activity-based and pupil-determined programmes of learning. Cooperation with other secondary schools and links with colleges of further education require more sophisticated organisation than the traditional school timetable. This challenges the easy control of the headteacher while imposing on all participants the requirement to specify aims and objectives of the programme and recognise the limitations which it may impose upon the well-ordered day of the conventional school curriculum.

Why careers education is needed

It is not only teachers of traditional humanities and creative subjects who feel threatened by the present emphasis on subjects that are vocationally relevant in a technological society, but for them the issues are most critical. Discussions in staffrooms explore the issue of vocational relevance versus personal development as though these were inherently dichotomous. All teachers are competing for scarce resources and for the backing of the headteacher and administrators responsible for the allocation of funds, equipment and staffing.

Careers education is thought by some to be irrelevant if pupils are sampling various prevocational fields through TVEI; other teachers consider the whole question of guidance and job knowledge to have been postponed because so many leavers are now entering the twilight zone of a Youth Training Scheme (YTS) and have two years of post-school trial employment experience. There is ample evidence, however, that from the age of thirteen, if not earlier, boys and girls are thinking about work and non-work and so need informed, structured provision of opportunities to consider their own future plans.

They are much more conscious of the world of work now that so many of them have parents who are unemployed and friends or older siblings who have not been able to get a job on leaving school. Moreover, they glimpse the working world through television programmes whereas previous generations depended upon their limited contacts through parents and neighbours. Country children can compensate for their disadvantages in having to travel considerable distances to attend a secondary school. They, perhaps, have a more limited range of curricular offerings, but they are usually more knowledgeable about what people in a village do for a living than their urban contemporaries, many of whom do not even know what their parents' jobs are – except those suffering the consequences of parental unemployment. Town children are more aware of the changing pattern of job opportunity from technological innovation, international trade which has killed whole industries in some areas, changing policies of governments and financial institutions which affect the balance between the public and private sectors of the economy and changes in popular fashion and leisure pursuits. The spread of ownership of computers and video recorders opens up endless prospects for modules of learning to be acquired at home and this will almost certainly include programs relating to job opportunities. Young people need appropriate training in techniques of information retrieval and decision taking if they are to use the new resources successfully. That presupposes an integrated system of careers education and guidance in every secondary school and recognition that all pupils need guidance as they develop their interests and abilities and prepare for the transition from school life to adult life.

Definitions

School governors and parents sometimes confuse the two groups of professional people concerned in careers work by referring to the *careers teacher* on the school staff as the careers officer. The *careers officer* is, of course, an official of the Local Education Authority (LEA) Careers Service who may have the use of an office in the school, but is more likely to be a visitor attending regularly in order to interview pupils at appropriate decision-taking points in their schooling or to assist the careers teacher in formulating and implementing a programme of careers events. The term *careers adviser* is used in this book wherever the function described may equally well be carried out by a careers teacher or careers officer.

Guidance implies the process by which the education of boys and girls is developed by a combination of classroom sessions and individual tutorial work. Pupils entering secondary schools need guidance about the new subjects they will be studying, the arrangements for pastoral care, the range of extra-curricular activities and the increasing responsibilities they will assume for their own education and development as pupils. Guidance is primarily the function of tutors, especially when it involves discussion of academic strengths which might indicate possible choices of higher education. It may be accomplished in groups or by individual tutorial. Sophisticated computerised systems are being introduced into guidance programmes whereby information banks are held in the computer and the software programs support the teacher when helping pupils to assess their interests, values and abilities.

Guidance is a useful umbrella term for the entire apparatus of information, encouragement and action to support pupils and their parents throughout the secondary years. *Careers guidance* is one aspect of the total guidance programme and consists of cognitive learning, skills acquisition and the gradual development of attitudes and understanding related to ideas about the working world. It is designed to help individual boys and girls to decide upon a selection of possible future occupations and also to help them to appreciate the aspirations of others.

Careers education is undertaken by teachers as an integral part of the curriculum (whereas careers guidance may be given by teachers or by careers officers who are specifically trained in interview techniques and have opportunities to acquire detailed knowledge of the requirements of courses and occupations at all levels). Careers education may start as early as the first year of the secondary-school course, but is normally found in the timetable from the third year. Representatives of the working world may be included in the programme which will frequently involve extra-mural activities. The influence of parents has to be acknowledged by regular consultation and occasional incorporation in the programme.

Counselling has not developed as rapidly in this country as was hoped by those who supported the setting up in 1966 of the first training courses for teachers anxious to become counsellors. It is essentially a means of augmenting the school's pastoral system by enabling pupils to discuss their personal or academic problems with a sympathetic adult, usually their tutor. Group counselling takes place in many schools and if there is a trained counsellor on the staff he or she may be introduced to classes as a preliminary to self-referral by those with a problem. Some counsellors work part-time as counsellors and part-time teaching their normal subject, but this poses many difficulties if the counsellor has to switch roles from sympathetic counsellor to classroom disciplinarian. Counselling is not needed by all pupils, though it should be known to be available at least through the tutorial system. *Careers counselling* is a term used by some careers teachers who do not teach classes of pupils but prefer to give careers information and guidance on a one-to-one counselling basis.

Opinions differ on the desirability of precise definitions of all these terms, but most professionals in the field agree that careers education should be a legitimate part of the main school curriculum and can justify its place as a 'subject', with the same elements of a body of knowledge to be acquired, skills to be practised and scope for discussion of values and ideals as many traditional academic subjects. Many pupils only require occasional guidance and limited counselling, especially when they are provided with a good programme of careers education.

In this book the word *careers* comprises the entire spectrum of occupations at all levels of education and skill whereas it has sometimes been used in opposition to 'job' and signifying progress up a ladder of promotion in a profession. It includes non-work activities such as voluntary work and homemaking and other lifestyles which may not include working for a wage or salary but various forms of self-employment and intervals of unemployment. Many practitioners have spent long hours of discussion to try to find a better term, but even the experienced careers teachers in the Schools Council TRACE project failed to find another word for this part of the school curriculum.

How to use this book

This book is divided into three parts. Part 1 argues that careers education and guidance are essential elements in the secondary-school course for boys and girls of all levels of ability and aspiration and that, therefore, provision must be made within the school for the evolution of a policy for implementing this belief. Part 2 contains the chapters outlining practical considerations of organisation, staffing, resources and external influences. Part 3 attempts to identify the main problems and constraints which affect the way in which a headteacher may approach decisions on developing the staff's contribution to the whole-school policy for careers across the curriculum and suggests criteria for evaluating its effectiveness.

Having accepted the thesis that all teachers are, in varying degrees, concerned in this aspect of the school's life, it is probably most productive of any necessary change in attitude or practice if the position of careers is made the subject of a staff development conference. A residential weekend can give scope for contributions from representatives of external agencies, such as the Careers Service or Manpower Services Commission, to provide factual information and lead discussions; but if this it not practicable, a one-day training day can be useful or a succession of short meetings to consider limited aspects of the whole topic. Whichever way is chosen, it will be important for the headteacher to be seen to support the principle and for as many colleagues as possible to be invited to contribute to specific parts of the discussion. It should not be left to the careers department to provide all the formal inputs. Any newly joined members of staff who have had recent experience of working in industry, commerce or other non-teaching roles can be particularly valuable. Staff should be asked to volunteer to lead discussion on those parts of the topic which especially interest or concern them; as many as possible should have been given the opportunity to read relevant parts of the book – even if they disagree with the tenor of its argument!

If one accepts the premise that careers has a fundamental place in the school curriculum it follows that some teachers must be appointed to take responsibility for it and in Chapter 6 the functions and position of careers teachers are delineated. The old adage that every teacher is a teacher of English can be rephrased as every secondary-school teacher is concerned with careers. The designation of a few members of staff as careers teachers does not excuse their colleagues from responsibility for certain aspects of the total process by which pupils achieve what the Americans call 'vocational maturity'. All teachers are involved as tutors with pastoral functions which include guidance and counselling, as organisers of activities which have a careers element or as teachers of subjects which are relevant to some pupils' career ambitions. Furthermore, all members of a secondary-school staff should be aware of the local employment background for which their charges are being prepared, however dismal it may be at a particular time. They should all be as concerned to develop leavers' employability as to foster other aspects of growing up into confident adulthood. It follows, then, that headteachers need to devote some time in their annual schedule of in-service training and staff meetings to topics associated with the position of the school in the surrounding community and its relationship to the local economy, whether agricultural, industrial or commercial.

This book is intended to provide headteachers with ideas for such staff development sessions, often in the form of issues for discussion as a preliminary to the formulation of some plan for the future advancement of the curriculum or extra-mural contacts. These topics and questions for debate have been grouped at the end of each Part because many are based upon more than one chapter.

Chapter 2

The Changing Pattern of Employment

Historical background

Many books have been written about the changes that have taken place in the way people earn a living, from the peasants toiling on the land in the Middle Ages through the growth of urban, factory work after the industrial revolution to the recent infusion of mechanisation, automation and, now, electronically controlled production operations. We are told that we are now in the post-industrial society, and visionaries even postulate a situation in which a quarter of the working population will be able to keep the rest in idleness. Put another way, Professor Tom Stonier of Bradford has forecast that by the turn of the century only 10 per cent of the people of working age will be producing all the goods and services we need.

When the primary sector of employment, agriculture, mining and quarrying, was the main source of employment in the early nineteenth century it occupied 85 per cent of the work force. Within a hundred years it declined to 15 per cent and now employs only 5 per cent of the working population. The growth of industries based upon coal, iron and steel, and the introduction of power looms in textiles and steam engines for transport are well documented. What is happening now, however, is entirely different. It is not the brawn of working men that is being replaced by machines, but their brainpower. If you look at the changes that have taken place in the years since the Second World War you wonder how futurologists dare attempt a detailed forecast of the likely pattern of employment in the twenty-first century, when pupils now in school will be seeking work.

A careers or social studies class can be taken through some of the main areas of human existence and prompted to discuss ways in which new inventions, materials or methods have altered the product and its related jobs: housing, with new materials and prefabricated systems; food processing and preservation which has revolutionised the life of housewives by enabling them to spend less time on domestic chores and so continue working; transport, particularly the invention of jet propulsion (and noting the decline of British manufacture of bicycles and motorcycles); energy and power from the building of nuclear-powered electricity generating stations to the replacement of coal and wood fires by central heating in the average home; clothing, particularly man-made fibres and drip-dry processing; health services enhanced by new pharmaceuticals and dramatic surgical techniques for replacing human organs; communications using satellites and the universal acceptance of colour television as the main form of domestic entertainment. One could go on, but the most important impact on job opportunities probably comes from the rapid installation of computers and microtechnology in industry and commerce.

It used to be a subject for debate whether the most important invention was the wheel, printing press, internal combustion engine or typewriter as regards their effect on our lives. The scientific innovations and technological applications of the last thirty years are likely to exert a far greater impact on human life and work than any of those four seminal discoveries.

The present

It is said that in the United States more than half the workers engaged upon the production and distribution of goods are working on products invented in the last fifty years. Now that English secondary schools have an average of fourteen microcomputers each and many pupils of primary-school age are practising keyboard skills with home computers or at school, there will soon be nothing more remarkable about the use of this skill than that of writing or reading. Some schools have encouraged pupils to take part in projects designed by the teachers of science and technology to construct small robots and gadgets to replace human musclepower and control them electronically. Robotisation is here to stay, and anyone who has been privileged to see the mind-boggling robots making robots in the Fujitsu Fanuc factory in Japan must be fearful for the employment prospects of those young people of limited ability and minimal educational attainments who may be hoping to obtain jobs in manufacturing industry.

There will never again be many jobs for men and women who have nothing to offer an employer except physical strength. This message must be impressed constantly upon teachers, parents and young people so that the undoubtedly higher general standards of education we have achieved can be accelerated to enable leavers to cope with the demands of the modern world. The misnamed agricultural labourer is now a highly skilled husbandman and mechanic responsible for manipulating expensive and complex machinery. Traditionally trained craftsmen in the engineering industry are now confronted by numerically controlled machines in computer-aided manufacturing systems which impose greater demands on their skills and attention.

The United Kingdom can only feed part of its population from home-grown foodstuffs and needs to import much of the raw material required by manufacturing industry. Imports have to be paid for by the export of finished goods or invisible services such as banking and insurance. Manufacturing industry has been overtaken as the main source of employment by service industries and, consequently, higher standards of education are demanded since there is little routine unskilled work in finance, administration, health and welfare. The less well-equipped of our school leavers must compete for jobs in distribution and catering where there are still jobs requiring lower levels of attainment. Higher standards of basic education will be needed in any case if people are to be capable of training for the new jobs which changing technology may create. An adaptable and intelligent work-force will be more than ever in demand in the future.

This country has produced many eminent scientists and engineers, but somehow we have often failed to capitalise upon notable inventions because of a lack of marketing skills or the will to invest in their development. Industrialists complain that the education system still places undue emphasis upon pure, rather than applied, sciences and that we are inhibited by unwillingness to learn unfamiliar but commercially useful languages. The standard of living of the entire population and the opportunity for longer education and a more satisfying old age depend upon the capacity of those in the work-force to keep Britain internationally competitive. The ease with which goods and services can now cross frontiers means we are in competition with the fast-developing economies of some countries in the Far East and the rapid industrialisation of parts of the Third World. We can no longer export manufactured goods, regardless of standard, in exchange for food and raw materials. People talk with pride about the hallmark 'Made in Britain', but the relative industrial decline of Britain has been going on for a hundred years and was documented in the early chapters of the Finniston Report *Engineering Our Future* (HMSO Command Paper No. 7794, 1980).

The particular problems for girls

Clerical, administrative and distributive jobs now take up a larger proportion of the working population than those requiring manual or machine operating. This means a greater demand for good standards of performance in literacy, oracy and numeracy, apart from specific educational requirements set by examining bodies in the professions. Technology is having its impact upon office work as much as industry; many of the low-level clerical operations which have provided work for girls are being replaced by machines of one sort or another: photocopiers, calculators and computer terminals are everywhere visible in offices and girls now need training in word-processing and other forms of VDU application. Direct debiting and electronic cash transfer at the point of sale will affect much work in the retailing world where so many youngsters get their first taste of work. The plastic money revolution has only begun to affect jobs, but it will not go away and, indeed, may be considered an advance in that it eliminates some of the boring jobs which were previously the lot of less gifted school-leavers. The labour market will need more managers and professionals and fewer routine office workers – a fact that has implications for education and guidance, and needs repeated explanation at meetings for parents.

Another factor to be considered in relation to girls' conventional aspirations is the probable decline in office work when many business and professional people will be able to do their work on a home computer and dictate their letters into a machine instead of commuting from suburbs into city centres where they have been supported by numerous secretaries and clerks. The pictures of a deserted Stock Exchange floor after the introduction of computerised trading information starkly demonstrated this point. Why should people travel to a big office building if they can work just as effectively as a broker or merchant by installing modern office equipment in a room at home? This trend should provide more opportunities for women in traditional office jobs to do the same.

The demand for greater mobility from the work-force has caused a particular difficulty for some business and professional men who may refuse promotion if it means relocating to another part of the country where there may be less chance for the wife to continue in her career. When so many girls chose traditional careers as teachers, nurses, clerical workers and saleswomen they could find a new job relatively easily after their husbands' move, but this is no longer the case.

The guidance given to girls at school used to be considered less important than the provision for boys because it was assumed that many teenage girls were not career motivated and merely sought a well-paid job (if they could get it) to fill the gap between leaving school and starting a family (it is maternity rather than marriage which takes women out of the labour market). The rising figures for divorce and separation, with the consequent increase in the proportion of single-parent families mostly headed by a woman, necessitate a very sensitive and exhaustive programme of careers education and guidance for both boys and girls so that each recognise the impact of child-rearing upon the total lifestyle of each parent. Child development courses in schools attract few boys despite the trend for more boys to study home economics and for girls to take craft, design and technology than was apparent a decade ago. Parent preparation should be part of the core curriculum of all pupils and linked with aspects of careers education so that both boys and girls are aware of the particular career problems of the majority of girls who will wish at some stage to become mothers. The effect of high unemployment on the opportunities for part-time work should be included.

The impact on education

Teachers may claim that since the statutory school-leaving age has been raised twice since the Second World War, and very many more young people are pursuing higher and further education, the productivity of the schools has been proven. The truth is, unfortunately, that the pace of demand upon skills and knowledge has grown faster than the extension of education whether by law or the trend to longer schooling. We are still not producing enough high-quality scientists, technologists and engineers to satisfy manufacturing industry and its associated research institutes, let alone the education system itself.

Employers complain that many school-leavers lack certain attributes required for success in employment, not only in terms of standards of attainment in communications and numeracy but in attitudes to work. Youngsters appear to have 'switched off' long before they leave school even if they have not been physically truanting from the school premises. Casualness, inability to work in a team or take personal responsibility, lack of energy, drive and initiative, and poor handwriting, spelling and speech, added to unwillingness to undertake the sometimes tedious task of learning a particular process or technique, are all cited as reasons for employers' disinclination to offer young people the chance to prove their

capacity to be trained as competent workers. One of the good results of
the Youth Training Scheme has been the evidence that some young
people with modest school attainments have proved capable of training
when given the chance, but teachers must realise that unskilled work
will not be available to absorb large numbers of boys and girls who may
leave school inadequately educated for our complex society.

New work patterns

The changing pattern of employment has to be viewed not only in the
light of technology and economics but of wholly new employment styles.
In future, people will not expect to work for a forty-hour week for a wage
or salary from a public or private employer, but for different lengths of
time and often for themselves. School pupils should be told of the
possibilities of part-time work (including flexitime and other arrangements of special value to parents of young children), job-sharing
between two people, self-employment (which is being encouraged
officially as a means of contributing flexibly to the economy), schemes
for earlier retirement, sabbatical leave to enable workers to have a break
for intellectual or physical refreshment, and a move towards shorter
hours.

Young people need help in understanding the reasons for high
unemployment so that they do not feel inadequate and guilty. It is no
fault of theirs that almost all western countries are suffering from a
decline in economic activity and low demand for labour. Tutors and
careers teachers give pupils instruction on how to obtain the various
benefits open to those without jobs, but it is more important that
teachers should ensure that youngsters have opportunities for sympathetic and positive discussion about the reasons for unemployment and its
particularly hard impact on the young.

Classes on lifeskills can give self-confidence and pride which young
people historically derived from starting work and thereby achieving
adult status. Professor John Dancy of Exeter University, writing in the
Oxford Review of Education (issue 44 no. 3, 1978), suggested discussion of
the 'strategies of consolation in literature and in life' and listed a number
of topics which might be appropriate for this kind of course: looking at a
person's total lifespan up to the role of grandparent and facing old age;
the causes of uemployment and how to cope with it; identifying the
ethics of work; job satisfaction and how to cope with a boring job;
various forms of useful voluntary work for oneself, the family or the

community; the values which give people confidence that they possess certain abilities and attributes even if they cannot be used in a job. This is all ideal material for tutorial work with sixth-formers and requires very little material or textbooks and worksheets. At the same time a programme can be instituted to develop practical competencies useful in adult life, such as first aid or gardening.

If there is going to be more leisure for most adults in the future pupils now at school need better preparation for using time in a purposeful and enjoyable way. Optimists believe that much of the work done by young people with minimal education in recent years was boring and even dehumanising, so the chance to exchange a dull job in a typing pool or metalwork shop for working for oneself or one's family should be encouraged. It certainly has to be stressed that unemployment is not only a problem facing the unqualified (though it is more likely for them), but it also affects those who have had a successful school career. Those who have had longer education and been more successful academically are, of course, likely to be better able to use their enforced leisure because they have more intellectual and creative resources. We should all press for increased community resources to provide the workshops, tools, allotments or whatever may be needed to enable the unemployed to make use of the aptitudes and interests they have cultivated at school or college.

It is especially important that the less successful leavers should not feel that school has prepared them for a divisive society in which the able and energetic have jobs and the less favoured do not. They all need to be told about the redundancy of managers and professional people and about various MSC-funded schemes to help them to re-enter the workforce. In this way careers education contributes to the comprehensive ethos of secondary schools and promotes understanding of the problem facing some parents.

Nearly one in ten of the working population is self-employed or working in a small cooperative. This is a fact worth emphasising, although it is obviously better for young people to start by working for an employer in order to get the appropriate experience and skills before starting up on their own. It is also worth stressing when talking to pupils and parents about subject options that more pupils should choose mathematics and physical sciences if a steady growth in the national economy is to be attained to generate more work and provide for the unemployed, since these are the people needed to further technological innovation and promote international competitiveness. There are, moreover, more jobs at each level of educational achievement for those with scientific aptitude. Whenever a physics laboratory is closed or a CDT department empty the school is losing an opportunity to give its pupils the best possible chance of getting employment. But not all pupils can take this route and some appear inevitably doomed to periods of unemployment throughout their adult lives.

Teachers have a responsibility to help them to understand that they can still be useful citizens even if they cannot get ordinary paid work and have to resort to self-generated activity or a community project. As Professor Gilbert Wrenn, who started the first counselling course at Keele University, once said: 'Work is what you do for yourself or for society, whether it is paid for or not'.

At a time of high unemployment there appears to be a contradiction in the increasing vocationalisation of secondary-school programmes with the introduction of MSC-funded schemes to promote integrated education, training and work experience for full-time school pupils. The Certificate of Prevocational Education (CPVE) was intended to encourage more sixteen year olds to remain in education at school or college and the Technical and Vocational Education Initiative provides resources to inject strands of work-related activity into the schooling of pupils from the age of fourteen. All this poses a challenge not only to careers and guidance teachers coping with the penetrating questions of pupils facing new choices, but also to headteachers trying to assess the value of different schemes on which to devote scarce resources.

Even the teacher's job is changing as a result of more experiential learning and greater use of extra-mural resources to enrich many parts of the curriculum. Teachers concerned about their less successful pupils complain that the entry requirements of so many occupations have risen dramatically in the last twenty years. When GCE was introduced almost all professions, except medicine, dentistry and veterinary science could be entered with an appropriate combination of 'O' levels, but they now require 'A' levels, if not a degree. When teachers accuse other professions of exercising a restrictive practice in the interests of existing practitioners they need reminding that their own could be entered after a two-year college course and 'O' level qualifications in the fifties, but now requires matriculating 'A' levels and three or four years of higher education. We are all, alas, in the same business of 'academic inflation'.

Chapter 3

A Whole-school Careers Policy

What happened to the leavers?

Secondary schools claim to be caring institutions and obviously exist for the benefit of their pupils, just as hospitals exist for the benefit of patients. If boys and girls spend five, six or seven years in a school and teachers maintain that they are working to develop the abilities, talents and interests of their pupils, then it is not unreasonable to suggest that something should be known and recorded about their destination when they walk out of the school gates for the last time. This is just as true now as it was when virtually all leavers were able to get a job as soon as they left school or college.

Some school halls still display honours boards on which the names of the most academically successful students who have gone on to university are painted in gold. Individual teachers often have a detailed knowledge of the destinations of many pupils for whom they had tutorial responsibility or close connection through some extra-curricular activity. Sadly, many know which of these youngsters are unlikely to get a real job after depending on the Youth Training Scheme for their initiation into the world of work. Staffroom gossip sometimes reveals that individual leavers have got unusual jobs such as the esoteric taxidermist or tree surgeon or when a boy has defied the sex-stereotype by becoming a secretary or a girl been apprenticed to a bricklayer. Just as those pupils who have been particularly notable in games or drama stand out in teachers' memories, so do those who have expressed unusual interests and ambitions or been persistent in their requests for advice and guidance on the next stage of their life.

It is regrettably true, however, that few schools have a complete record of the immediate destiny of their leavers and still fewer keep in touch with them long enough to know whether they can be considered successful in whatever training course, further education or job they embarked upon. Boarding public schools seem to inspire a greater loyalty than maintained day schools in that old boys' and old girls' associations publish magazines giving accounts of job changes, qualifications acquired, promotions or other distinctions. Outsiders might maintain that a comprehensive school fails to live up to its claim to be a caring institution if it does not have a policy of guidance throughout the pupils' school career and some system for recording the outcomes of the education and advice given. Not only does this encourage the teachers concerned, but it enables information to be fed back to future generations enquiring about the connection between certain elements in the curriculum and the introduction to adult roles in the working world.

Some teachers quarrel with the notion that schools are educating young people for employment, but pupils and parents expect schooling to lead to a good job by whatever criterion that may be defined. Teachers rightly consider they are educating the whole person for his or her adult life. In some schools the emphasis is on producing good citizens or caring parents, inculcating moral or ethical principles (which may be dictated by the religious foundation of the school) or dedicated to the pursuit of scholarship and flowering of creative talent. None of these has any necessary connection with the future occupations of leavers. Certainly teachers are not expected to be primarily concerned to produce future clerks, technicians, managers or any other category of worker. There are some teachers who object to any suggestion that pupils are being conditioned to accept a particular form of society with its class distinctions and emphasis upon examinations or career success. But so long as parents hope schooling will lead to a good job, headteachers will want to assure them that the programme of education offered does take account of this desire and contains elements designed specifically to develop 'vocational maturity' and readiness to accept the responsibilities of adult working life.

Schools are expected to have policies on, for example, equal opportunity or health and safety; governors can legitimately ask for a statement of the school's policy on guidance. This should be clearly delineated, available to parents and formulated after appropriate staff consultation. It is not sufficient simply to provide for one of the teachers to be designated careers teacher, careers counsellor or guidance teacher since this of itself will achieve nothing unless that teacher has adequate time and resources and a clear idea of how the job should be done.

Formulating whole-school policies

It would be impossible to produce a universal blueprint for a whole-school policy on careers because schools vary so much. Some are conditioned by a long history and traditions, by the socio-economic background of the pupils or by the physical environment in which the school is located. Any school's educational philosophy changes from time to time as a result of staffroom discussions, policies suggested by the education authority or the arrival of a new headteacher with ideas of change which commended themselves to the governors who appointed him or her. Two apparently similar schools in the same area may have opposing philosophies on the relative importance of the academic curriculum or pastoral provision, or on the need for examination successes. They may differ on the proportion of resources devoted to particular groups of pupils such as those who in pre-Warnock days were in special schools, representatives of ethnic minorities and those who have to contend with disabilities or disadvantages. The policy may be affected by the extent to which the school practises mixed-ability teaching, team teaching or the rigid adherence to the timetable or a modular system with blocked time for special activities (which can be especially helpful to certain methods of careers education). The size of classes, access to external resources and flexibility with which teachers in different departments collaborate also affect the development of whole-school policies. 'Careers across the Curriculum' should be as commonly accepted as 'Language across the Curriculum'.

While there is high unemployment among young people teachers sometimes question whether time should legitimately be spent on any form of careers education and guidance. The pressures of other new subjects, such as health education, computer studies or political education and peace studies compete with the established areas of the curriculum for time which is often severely constrained. It is unlikely that an inspector would nowadays find a headteacher openly refusing to allow any time or facilities for careers education, but there are still many who clearly do not consider it important, judging by the provision they make. In fact, the worsening employment prospects for young people leaving full-time education at sixteen, eighteen or twenty-one can be regarded as a reason for *more* careers education rather than less because pupils and students need extra help in acquiring the necessary knowledge and skills to manage their transition into adulthood.

Curriculum guidance

In the days when schools offered a limited curriculum and most did not attempt to educate the full ability range there were often few choices presented; boys and girls were expected to take a set pattern of subjects until they reached the leaving age. Those in selective grammar schools were usually advised to study the subjects which would equip them for entry to a university or training for one of the professions. In coeducational schools an automatic division put the boys into classes on woodwork, metalwork and technical drawing while the girls did cookery, needlework and home economics. Now with a choice of some twenty subjects and a growing conviction that pupils should be encouraged to choose those subjects which attract them, it is clear that they need some guidance if they are to choose sensibly.

American high schools have for many years maintained an elaborate apparatus of counselling and guidance to help students find their way through the maze of choices which provide more freedom to sample areas of educational experience than is common in even the largest English comprehensive schools. The system is so much more flexible in any case that the consequences of decisions made in early teenage years have less drastic effect upon later educational opportunity or career choice. For years we have watched movements to broaden the curriculum in England and Wales, but older teachers may be forgiven for viewing AS levels with scepticism when so many attempts to broaden the curriculum of sixth-formers have failed in the past.

Manifestly there must be some method whereby pupils and parents can be guided through the educational decisions they normally have to make when boys and girls are thirteen and fifteen. As these educational choices affect and are affected by career choices and in many cases close vocational doors there is a strong case for guidance to start before the stage of the first option choices. Some schools start the guidance process from the age of entry whether eleven or, after a middle-school stage, at twelve or thirteen; in the latter case it will depend upon close collaboration between the various schools to avoid hasty decisions made from ignorance or misunderstanding.

Pastoral responsibilities

Apart from the obvious visible differences between schools, they also vary considerably in ethos. In some the discipline is explicit and accepted, in others an apparently casual attitude and behaviour may not be detrimental to high academic standards. Pastoral systems vary as do the arrangements by which teachers are chosen to exercise these responsibilities. When a house system is changed to a year system there will be different ways of providing support for pupils in need. The resources available for pastoral care vary from extensive accommodation in year and house rooms, well-equipped offices for the pastoral heads and time set aside within the teaching week for tutorial lessons and individual interviews with pupils and parents. In other schools there may be no visible provision and pastoral functions are carried out in laboratories, workshops, studios and classrooms by teachers with the bare minimum of time and training.

The amount of teacher time devoted to non-instructional contact with pupils is normally decided by the management of the school after general staff consultation. It will affect, among other things, the chances pupils have to discuss ideas about their future with a teacher whom they happen to like. We all know that youngsters have strong likings and antipathies for certain members of staff and often continue to consult a trusted teacher in whose class or tutor group they were placed at an earlier stage, even if they now have no formal contact with them. The pastoral system of a school is bound to have an influence upon the way a school adopts a policy for educational and vocational guidance. Tutor periods may be crucial to its implementation.

Not only is it more important nowadays that pupils get good careers education to help them overcome the results of economic recession and declining job vacancies, but they also need during adolescence to study the relationship between the economy, social structure and work because they ought to have a basic understanding of how wealth is created no matter what career they are hoping to follow themselves. This does not mean that they should all study economics as an examination subject but that they should have classroom discussion about the ways people earn their living and how workplaces are organised. They need to appreciate the connection between a person's occupation and total lifestyle, and the formal guidance programme should include elements on non-work such as homemaking, voluntary and community service, or the pursuit of creative and leisure activities without financial reward.

Tutorial periods can be used to discuss why people work, and the ways in which human labour supports the economy and satisfies people's needs for goods and services. Much of this can be taught by teachers whose main task is to teach a conventional subject, but who may have a particular interest, experience or ability which makes them especially suitable to contribute to the total careers programme in tutor periods. To be successful, this diffusion of careers education modules through tutors depends upon an enthusiastic and committed head of careers providing material and ideas to the tutors. Lively discussions have been observed in home economics classes on concepts of standard of living and the effect of work upon home life. An art studio decorated with the results of a project on people at work can lead to endless discussion.

Every secondary school teacher must be aware of some pupils whose lives have been deeply influenced by contact with him or her. It is no derogation to specialist careers teachers to point out that in the case of a musically gifted pupil it is the music teachers who can advise on applications to music academies more convincingly than the careers or pastoral team; only the musicians are likely to be able to assess that youngster's talent and potential against nationwide competition. The same is true in other subjects. There are many happy and successful workers at all levels of employment who owe their job satisfaction to the advice and encouragement given by an influential teacher during their secondary school years. *A policy for careers education and guidance should involve all teachers in the school.*

Attitudes of teachers

Few senior teachers have themselves experienced a good course of careers education at school. They are, of course, the successes of the system who passed examinations at regular intervals and found such personal fulfilment, interest and satisfaction in their chosen area of academic or practical study that they decided to pass on their enthusiasm to the next generations. Their love of a subject is understandable and, for many, the only way to continue its study is to teach it. Many teachers, therefore, fail to appreciate why other young people ought to have an element in their education which they themselves seemed never to need. Their own decision to continue in higher education the study of a favourite subject was probably confirmed by a brief interview with a careers officer and some guidance from the sixth-form tutor on applications to university or college.

There is a discernible difference between those teachers who view any connection with the world of work as adulterating the pure well of academic water in which their pupils are swimming (or floundering) and those who believe that microtechnology will soon remove the necessity to work for most of the population. Yet another group have never grasped the purport of careers education as an element in the curriculum and separate from individual careers guidance.

In some schools the careers teacher is barely visible as such because he or she has no timetabled careers periods, the subject is not taught formally at all and the teacher is little more than custodian of the books and pamphlets on occupations which arrive from time to time. Some colleagues apparently believe that the careers teacher has a soft option sitting in a little room talking to individual pupils and parents or, even more enviably, getting out of school to visit colleges and employers while they cope with classes of reluctant scholars. While there may be general recognition in the staffroom that statutory age school-leavers may need help in getting placed in a YTS scheme, they consider that the province of the Careers Service and no concern of the school. Other teachers who have mainly taught the academically successful assume that they need little help because their careers will be dictated by the courses they will take at university where a careers advisory service will cope with any problems they may have later on. There is plenty of evidence that the most academic pupils get the least careers education and guidance, so a whole-school policy must embrace pupils of all levels of academic ability and teachers be convinced of this, however distasteful or disruptive it may appear to them.

One may sympathise with the hard-pressed teacher who wants the maximum time on the timetable for his or her subject in order to get the examination passes necessary for those pupils who want to get into degree courses. But there is another attitude which is sometimes expressed in staffrooms where some teachers genuinely believe that the environment of some occupations is such that they would not encourage any of their pupils to go to such places. This contention is often based upon deeply held convictions about the nature of capitalism and may be expressed vociferously as, 'We don't want careers education in this school if it is going to turn our boys and girls into factory fodder for a capitalist society'. One argument can be that when jobs are scarce a good programme of careers education should help pupils to choose wisely and share out the available jobs among those most suitable for them. Furthermore, we live in an interdependent society where all benefit from the labour of others. Many teachers might not want to work on a building site, in a food factory, sewing garments or making automobile parts, but we all live in houses, wear manufactured clothes and eat prepared food and most of us drive cars. The logical argument is, therefore, that so long as we enjoy consuming the products of industrial labour we are hypocritical to try to stop our leavers from working in industry.

The case for careers education

Careers education is a vital part of the education of all boys and girls. At one time the choice of a career was the most important choice any young person made apart from the choice of a spouse. For many youngsters nowadays the bitter fact is that there may not be a career at all in the accepted sense of lifetime employment in a reasonably satisfying job. But for others it is still a reality affecting their intellectual, emotional and character development. It is a chance to use aptitudes, abilities and talents, to exercise responsibility and be of service to others, to influence people and affairs in public service, the media and helping professions, to travel and to enjoy a wide range of social contacts.

Careers education can be an exciting part of the curriculum of quite young children; classes of eleven and twelve year olds enjoy as much as primary-school pupils studying 'a day in the life of...' and similar projects. It must start in the third year when options are being chosen for the two-year run up to GCSE. Some schools arrange elaborate occasions when pupils and parents are issued with booklets outlining the various subjects and combinations available and then meet members of staff from each department. This is sometimes followed by a careers convention so that they can discuss their choices with representatives of various occupations. Some people object to this, however, on the grounds that young people may be unduly influenced to take subjects they believe to be useful for a career they fancy at that stage when other subjects might be better for their personal development and long-term future. Careers education must include practice in decision making and some attention to self-assessment if pupils are to choose subjects in the light of their strengths and weaknesses as well as interests.

At sixteen boys and girls have to make mutually exclusive choices between staying at school, transferring to a college or leaving for work or a YTS programme. These choices will be made more knowledgeably if the pupils have worked through classes to compile a survival kit containing their curriculum vitae, some profiles of achievements, information on resources in the community to help in getting training and work, and model letters and application forms, all of which may come in useful at a later stage.

While a whole-school policy for careers involves most teachers and all pupils it must take account of the problems of certain groups of young people – the disadvantaged economically; pupils from homes where customs, languages and attitudes may be different from school; girls who refuse to take careers classes seriously or to achieve at the level of their academic potential; those who live in rural areas, seaside towns or inner city areas of declining job opportunities; low achievers from affluent homes; and able youngsters whose background may be antipathetic to the idea of prolonged education. Special efforts may be needed to give these young people the necessary stepping stones to occupational entry and success. If there are no jobs for most of them it should at least have given them self-confidence and be linked with other subjects to promote the acquisition of life-skills and competencies together with a robust philosophy, whether based upon religious beliefs or not. Without careers education in school many will be dependent upon occasional contacts with a careers officer or the social services. When schools adopt a policy for careers and make good provision for it headteachers can feel they have exercised their proper responsibility in helping young people to face the future with hope and confidence, however bleak it may appear at the time. All subject teachers occasionally feel they are battling against their colleagues for time and resources; careers teachers especially need the headteacher's support to provide a programme of work to match the developing needs of their pupils as they approach the successive decisions they have to make on future education and employment.

Chapter 4
Aims and Objectives

Guidance is conventionally divided into personal, educational and vocational. There may be good reasons for this when one considers some discussions which take place between pupils and teachers, but it is unrealistic to presuppose too discrete a distinction between these elements because they inevitably often overlap and one leads to another. A boy may ask the careers teacher an apparently simple question on the qualifications to enter the Merchant Navy, for instance, and the teacher hands over an appropriate leaflet. If that teacher has time for a proper interview, however, it may transpire that the underlying reason for the lad's enquiry is that the only career that he can think of which would enable him to leave home is the traditional one of running away to sea. A sensitive teacher may then convert what appears to be a straightforward request for factual information into a genuine counselling interview in an attempt to solve what is basically a personal problem arising from a breakdown of relationships in the boy's home. Similarly a question about entry to some form of higher education may, if the teacher has time to probe deeper, reveal that the girl was asking about degree courses hoping the discussion would lead to a private talk about a sense of vocation she feels to be a missionary or some other way of fulfilling her ideals in an occupation which shyness and fear of ridicule prevents her from airing in public classes.

So, if we accept that interviews can often span the whole spectrum of personal, educational and vocational guidance, we can attempt to define the objectives which may highlight a distinction between the specific tasks of designated careers teachers and the more general guidance given by tutors. One example is the responsibility for advice and guidance to candidates for degree courses. This has traditionally been the function of sixth-form tutors, but devolves upon subject department heads in some instances and is linked to the careers teachers in others. Sometimes there is an apparent divorce between those teachers responsible for advice on higher education and those dealing with careers guidance so that pupils may have to consult one teacher after another in order to get answers about graduate careers. Collaboration is obviously essential.

Definitions of aims and objectives

Several definitions have been published in recent years, but there is fairly general agreement that the aims and objectives of careers work in secondary schools can be grouped under four headings. At their most succinct these are:

(a) to develop educational awareness through knowledge of the courses available in schools and colleges and an understanding of the relationship between the career choices a student may make and the educational requirements for entry to them;

(b) to provide information on the whole spectrum of possible occupations with an understanding of the difference between the existence of a career (such as ballet dancer) and the limited opportunities for pursuing it; at the same time students should learn to appreciate the lifestyles associated with different types of work and non-work;

(c) to develop self-awareness through understanding of individual abilities and competencies (one's own as well as others'), of interests which may be relevant and the ideals and values which may motivate people to a particular course of action; students should also acquire an appreciation of those qualities of personality and character which may lead to success in achieving one's educational and career aspirations;

(d) to provide practice in decision-making and develop the necessary skills for coping with the transition from school to work, non-work, continued education and the services available to help them; understanding the social and economic background to work and a survival kit for immediate use or to cope with later job changes and re-entry to the workforce after a gap.

When is guidance needed?

Manifestly some pupils mature earlier than others and any policy established by the school must take account of this. Some timetable should be laid down, however, so that the essential topics are covered within a course of careers education or personal and social development.

At the same time pupils must have sufficient opportunity to have guidance and counselling if they have a crisis at home or in school. Some members of the careers team should be available for this type of crisis counselling at stated times each day. The careers officers do not usually take such a prominent part in this process as they did when many of them spent a day or two each week in school; this was especially helpful in schools where there was no formal timetabled careers education and teachers had had little training in careers work. The careers office is normally open after the school day finishes and, of course, when schools are closed for the holidays so no youngster needs to be without access to information on courses and careers when need arises.

Schools have usually set up a system of educational guidance at times when pupils make decisions on the subjects they are going to take at the next stage in their schooling and it is disturbing to hear some adults claim that they were not helped at school, took unpalatable subjects or found themselves on the wrong course or in an unsuitable job. Perhaps teachers do not sufficiently appreciate the dilemma facing thirteen year olds obliged by the system to make choices which will inevitably have consequences on their future lives and opportunities. Teachers ought to welcome the erosion by MSC programmes of the traditional apprenticeship system which forced nearly half the boys in many schools to leave at sixteen when they might have preferred or benefited by another year or two of full-time education, but were cast upon the rough seas of industry in the mistaken belief that a lifetime's security would be achieved by serving time in a skilled craft or trade. Careers officers explaining the age restrictions of apprenticeship to pupils and parents sometimes made themselves unpopular in school staffrooms where teachers correctly believed that the long-term interests of many pupils would be better served by continued education. This could result in an unfortunate lack of confidence between fifth-form tutors and careers advisers conscious of the race against time for those boys wanting to train for a manual skill.

Educational guidance starts at the induction stage when pupils arrive at their secondary school from a junior or middle school. Guided parental choice may have replaced the traumas of eleven-plus selection, but headteachers still have to explain to parents the various subjects offered in the school and other aspects of its ethos and organisation. Parents need to know whether uniform is obligatory, what system of rewards and punishments operates, whether pupils are banded, setted or streamed for certain subjects, at what stage additional languages can be started or new subjects introduced into the curriculum, and so on. More than that, parents need guidance on the pastoral structure and arrangements if they are to be confident that their children will be properly cared for in a big school.

Many boys and girls have stated career ambitions from the age of ten or younger and, although they may change as reality replaces fantasy in their aspirations, some of them remain remarkably consistent. The obviously important stage at which guidance is required is, however, when at thirteen or fourteen they are confronted with the necessity to choose subjects for the two-year course leading to GCSE. Those educational decisions should be made in the light of their possible vocational consequences. Too often youngsters choose subjects because they like the teacher or want to be with a friend or wrongly believe that the subject will be useful to them later on. Third-year tutors must be alert to the need to ensure a balanced curriculum for all pupils, but also see that occupational doors are not slammed in their faces at a later stage because they lack an important subject, often a physical science. The really vital stage is, of course, when pupils are sixteen and face the mutually exclusive decision to stay at school, move into further education or try for a job or training. Here, careers officers will be ready to reinforce the guidance given by careers teachers and fifth or sixth-form tutors.

A programme for careers

The most obvious way for these aims and objectives to be achieved is by establishing a programme of identifiable careers education with a teacher responsible for its implementation. At the same time, a whole-school policy on careers education and guidance implies that all teachers working with teenagers are involved in it and are aware of their part in that programme. If, as one hopes, many other teachers are going to participate in the total process of guidance they must know how their part fits into the overall aims and objectives while these must themselves consort with the total aims and objectives of the school. This may cause a dilemma if, for example, a policy of maximum examination entry to equip pupils with the widest choice of further and higher education so fills the time available that no classroom work in careers is timetabled; pupils will be dependent on tutorial periods for guidance and the cognitive part of careers education. This can be done, but it is not as satisfactory as a proper timetabled careers curriculum.

In some schools careers education is entirely diffused throughout the pastoral curriculum and tutors work through the material provided by the designated careers teachers. This does not work if the tutorial periods are taken up with individual pupils' problems and ideas because there is a general corpus of knowledge to be acquired if pupils are to finish their fifth year with adequate coverage of the topics listed in the aims of the careers department. In other instances tutorial discussions are used to complement a formally structured programme of set careers lessons taken by the specialist teachers.

The objectives can be achieved by parcelling out elements of the programme to different departments in the school, leaving the tutors to tackle the more personal guidance and counselling which some pupils may from time to time need. That will be outlined later. It presupposes general staff recognition that all pupils need practice in decision making, self-assessment and knowledge of the educational and vocational future which may await them and that someone undertakes to give them the planning skills for leaving school. If all teachers accept this premise the headteacher will find it easy to implement the policy by one means or another. If not, then the careers teachers will be fighting a battle for time and resources for themselves and their pupils; they may even find themselves competing with pastoral colleagues for the trust and confidence of pupils facing crisis points requiring guidance. The aims and objectives of a whole-school policy in this field can only be achieved by general recognition of its importance and willingness to participate.

Making it work

People sometimes ask by what criteria one can assess whether the accepted aims and objectives have been achieved. It is not possible to claim success if all pupils get into higher and further education or employment because there are too many factors making that impossible nowadays. A languages teacher might say that the first objective of that department had been achieved if all pupils could read French with understanding, and write and speak the language comprehensibly; but most teachers of French would claim that they hope in addition to give pupils a grasp of the historical and economic background to French literature. To have a three-course meal on the table at one o'clock on a Sunday might be considered the objective of a cookery class, but no home economist would be satisfied with that.

Some teachers may not readily accept the need for a statement of the aims and objectives of a careers department nor of a whole-school policy for careers teaching just because they themselves felt no need for the kind of experiences which are now being included in careers work. They probably had an easy path to the realisation of their ambitions, but things are very different now, even for young teachers leaving their training. For most young people the more flexible pattern of education, training and retraining against a background of high unemployment means they need more help while still in school to mount a chosen workhorse. Teachers are well aware of the problem, especially if they admit to relative good fortune in having a job which gives them reasonable satisfaction and comparative security despite declining promotion prospects as a result of falling rolls. A policy for establishing agreed aims and objectives for careers education has to be evolved in consultation with all members of staff if most of them are to take part in its implementation. A brief consideration of the ingredients of its four aspects will demonstrate that no single teacher (or even a department of two or three) can easily succeed compared with whole-staff discussion. Such cooperation should lead to many colleagues volunteering to bring to it their individual interests, capacities and experience.

Topics for staff discussion

1. Is there an anti-industrial bias in British secondary schools? Does it matter and if so what can teachers do about it?
2. Should schools actively prepare pupils for employment?
3. Do prevocational and foundation courses justify their place in the curriculum of pupils aged fourteen to eighteen?
4. TVEI is said to be putting the clock back by stressing the 'useful' elements in education. Is this true and, if so, good or bad?
5. How can a school make most use of its connections with the surrounding community?
6. Work experience, sampling, shadowing and observation are now accepted parts of the programme for many pupils. How can they be introduced/extended?
7. What impact has YTS had upon the school? Has the sixth form suffered and how can this be avoided?
8. How can teachers working in areas of high unemployment help pupils whose parents are unemployed and who have little hope of a job themselves when they leave?
9. How much can distance learning, video recording, TV and new forms of experiential learning affect conventional teaching methods and how can best use be made of them to enhance pupils' curriculum as preparation for adult life?
10. Is the school's guidance system adequate?
11. Should the school do more to involve parents in the total guidance programme? If so, how?
12. Some teachers claim that careers work is not needed in school because of the high unemployment. How can it be justified among competing demands for curriculum time and resources?
13. Does the school make sufficient provision for counselling of individual pupils with problems? How would other members of staff cope with examples cited by volunteers?
14. What experience of work outside teaching have staff members had? Can this contribute to the careers programme in any way?
15. How can we raise overall standards of education to enable leavers to cope with the demands of an increasingly complex society?
16. How should teachers combat sex-stereotyping of career ambitions and encourage girls to widen their occupational horizons, prepare for a dual-career role as workers and mothers and the possibility of becoming the family breadwinner?

17. Which teachers can contribute to the teaching of practical life-skills and competencies?
18. Should tutorial periods be used to give pupils understanding of the background to unemployment, wealth creation, use of leisure and interdependence of work and workers?
19. By what means can a school prepare pupils for possible future self-employment and running their own business?
20. Is the options system unnecessarily restrictive?
21. Should the school's record system be extended to note entry to employment or training and subsequent success in qualifying professionally?
22. Is the pastoral structure as effective as it might be in helping pupils to prepare for adult and working life? Is a year system preferable to houses and should teachers remain with the same group for five years or rotate?
23. How do we identify those pupils who have special needs for guidance?
24. What is the most effective way of providing advice on higher education?
25. Do all staff support the head of careers' definition of the aims and objectives of guidance and careers work?
26. What part can every teacher play in implementing a whole-school policy of careers and guidance for pupils of all levels of academic ability?

PART II
PRACTICALITIES

Chapter 5

Implementing a Policy for Careers

Two assumptions can be made with some confidence. First, for most boys and girls careers education will not be a formal part of their education until they reach the secondary school, though some primary schools provide experiences which might be considered part of elementary careers work when, for example, a class of children studies a day in the life of a postman, farmer or sales assistant. Secondly, most schools provide some guidance at the point when pupils have to choose subjects in preparation for public examinations at sixteen and arrange for some consideration to be given at that stage to any career ideas the pupils may have expressed. Beyond that there is great variety.

Boys and girls in the first year or two of secondary school often have romantic ideas about future careers and can be heard discussing the possibilities of becoming space pilots or deep sea divers. They are at what psychologists call the fantasy stage of vocational maturity. Teachers should not dismiss this stage too readily because some youngsters stick resolutely to an ambition and are thus motivated to higher scholastic or creative achievement than anyone might have predicted. Medicine is known to be a career often successfully pursued by people who first expressed a desire to be a doctor at the fantasy stage; on the other hand, few of the relatively large number of girls who say they want to be vets when asked about their future actually pursue the necessary science subjects for entry to this highly competitive training.

Eleven and twelve year olds

In some schools the first formal careers education occurs when a careers teacher talks to junior assemblies on a year or house basis to prepare them for the introduction of a guidance element in the next stage. Sometimes these young pupils are given an introduction to the careers library at that stage, too. This can awaken latent curiosity about occupations and inspire confidence that the school will be providing specific preparation during the middle and upper school stages for choice of subject and careers.

Apart from the obvious role of tutors in responding to the occasional request for information or reassurance, much good work is achieved by teachers of home economics and social studies who may include aspects of life and social skills in their classes with younger pupils. It is rare for 'careers' to appear on the timetable of pupils below the third year, but careers teachers can help tutors by injecting elements into tutor periods to foster interest in looking at adult roles and lifestyles as a base on which to build more structured careers classes in the middle-school years.

Educational guidance

Even in schools which have not adopted a general policy of careers education for all pupils of every ability and talent, there is generally recognition of the need for educational guidance at the stage when pupils are choosing subjects from a list of options for the two-year course leading to GCSE and Scottish 'O' grades. Schools all offer some curricular choices at this stage, whether pupils are entering for public examinations or not. Boys and girls manifestly need guidance here, not only on the likelihood of their coping with the demands of particular areas of the curriculum but on the need to have a balanced programme including languages, sciences, humanities and aesthetic subjects.

Tutors have often had to deal with one or two youngsters who have difficulties with some parts of their curriculum or find their classmates incompatible or are prevented by some crisis at home from making the most of their schooling. That is part of the counselling function of tutors. The more strictly educational guidance element occurs when pupils are choosing subjects; here the philosophy of the school and its curricular structure will dictate the way in which such guidance is provided. Obviously, the tutors can be expected to know something of the academic ability and potential of the individual pupils in their groups, but constraints on staffing and resources which affect choices may only be apparent to those at the top of the school hierarchy who have to reconcile competing claims for accommodation, staff and materials. Tutors have to face these constraints when helping their charges to choose a curriculum which fosters appropriate personal and intellectual development and makes the most of their abilities and capacities.

While the educational guidance of thirteen years olds must take account of their differing ability levels it may have to be undertaken against a background of inadequate assessment or record-keeping. It will be particularly difficult if the school has a policy of mixed ability teaching and it is less easy to see which pupils are notably good at certain subjects. Since the choice of subjects at thirteen has such consequences for later choice of career, tutors need reminding that other aspects than the purely academic must be considered. Scholastic potential may reasonably be assessed from termly reports by subject teachers, but creative and practical abilities may be just as relevant to the successful development of a young person's capacity as the more obvious intellectual strengths and weaknesses. Tutors will need to note qualities of personality, temperament and character and ensure that artistic, musical, dextrous and atheletic boys and girls have the same opportunities for development as those who manifest potential for high achievement in mathematics, sciences or languages. Profiling helps to identify qualities which may be more relevant to future training and employment than traditional examination passes and is certainly a useful supplement to them.

Technical and Vocational Education Initiative

The Technical and Vocational Education Initiative (TVEI) has expanded rapidly from its birth at the end of 1982 and now provides an exciting opportunity for schools to infuse the curriculum with elements relevant to the world of work. It has clear implications for the educational guidance of pupils entering a programme from the age of fourteen to eighteen and is designed to equip them with skills and knowledge which may be useful when they embark upon a career. New options on electronics, technology, robotics, food science, biotechnology, agricultural technology, business studies and information technology, for example, impose fresh responsibilities on tutors guiding thirteen year olds. Headteachers have to find ways of infusing the curriculum of all pupils with elements of computer-aided learning and links with the outside world. The scheme is designed to include careers and educational guidance and counselling, work experience and activities to develop initiative, teamwork and problem solving. Many TVEI schemes emphasise personal and social skills as well as economic awareness, and bring the world of work into the school by the addition of links with local industries, simulations and mini-enterprises to give pupils a foretaste of the real world of industry and commerce.

It is vital that pupils of a wide range of abilities take part in TVEI activities and also that its emphasis on practical applications of skills does not mean that academic highflyers are excluded. Tutors undertaking educational guidance have a new and exciting opportunity in schools that have wholeheartedly embraced the concepts of TVEI. It has obvious connotations for the work of those teachers in the careers department who will be working closely with the local area or school TVEI coordinator.

Careers guidance

While educational guidance is generally accepted as a function of the pastoral and academic structure of the school and often undertaken primarily by tutors and year heads, it is not always recognised that careers guidance needs some specific and formal programme within the timetable and cannot satisfactorily be left to a counselling interview with a tutor or careers officer. There are many permutations of systems of organisation for careers education once a policy has been accepted that all pupils need a proportion of their school time devoted to this part of preparation for adult life. At one end of the spectrum all pupils in years three, four and five (two, three and four in Scotland) receive a weekly period for careers classes which may include modules of health education, political education, religious education, history, geography, social studies, English and mathematics. The weekly period (or its equivalent in blocked periods to facilitate extra-mural activities) allows the careers teachers to cover the major topics required to implement the agreed aims and objectives of careers education. Where schools operate a forty-period week, this takes up 2·5 per cent of pupils' time – an equation which can be used to form the criterion for quantifying the careers education in other forms of organisation such as carousels of blocked afternoons for half-terms alternating with other subjects such as health education.

Some schools endeavour to put all the careers education in tutorial time and provide the careers teachers with sufficient non-teaching time to enable them to prepare worksheets and material, reading lists, film and video resources and other support to the tutors. I have encountered schools with as many as thirty-six teachers attempting a significant part of the formal, cognitive part of the careers programme, a system which imposes tremendous strains upon the head of careers because it is unlikely that all these teachers show equal interest in the subject or capacity to interest the pupils. It is depressing to watch bored youngsters working their way solidly through piles of worksheets or lackadaisically acting out a role-playing exercise on interviews.

It is an advantage for the careers teachers to be exempted from the rota of form tutors so that they can visit different tutor groups in turn or conduct large-scale exercises in year or house assemblies. This is not easy for even experienced careers teachers because pupils should be able to work at differing paces and undertake cooperative projects. It is also important that those youngsters who think they have already made sensible plans for their future should enjoy their careers lessons as a way of understanding more about the adult world and how people's work inter-relates rather than merely as a means of deciding on their own future. This is essential to the true implementation of a policy for careers education, especially in areas of high youth unemployment. Pupils switch off very rapidly if they are not interested in a subject they believe irrelevant to their own concerns.

In some schools the careers teachers are timetabled for careers, but not the pupils, so classes are assembled on the basis of withdrawal from timetabled subjects such as English or games. This system is justified by its advocates on the grounds of flexibility, but it is difficult to retain the interest of pupils in topics which occur only one week in four or five and most experienced careers teachers prefer to have blocks of time if they are not allowed to teach careers on a weekly basis. It is, moreover, very difficult for pupils in a withdrawal system to have access to computerised guidance systems which are dependent upon batch processing to a mainframe computer because they will not have continuity or the necessary overall time to complete the exercises. The simple input of a questionnaire into the terminal can produce a factual answer to a request for information on subjects and levels required for an occupation, but it cannot provide any self-assessment based on the use of inventories. This requires regular and consistent classroom work if it is to be profitable.

In some areas the unfortunate connotation of the word 'careers' with middle-class occupations or ladders of promotion has led some teachers to advocate teaching careers under some other title such as social education, integrated humanities, social studies or the fashionable personal and social development. This may ensure that pupils receive preparation for adult life, but it has the disadvantage of risking the disappearance of the subject if some new policy on, say, social education is implemented which requires the whole of the timetabled time for the year. A genuine case can be made for 'careers' to appear on the timetable and for headteachers to assure parents, governors and inspectors that adequate provision has been made for all pupils to have appropriate preparation for adult and working life.

By describing some schools' methods of implementing a policy of careers education and guidance I do not suggest any 'best buy' since these are illustrations rather than models and circumstances will determine the best way for each school to work out its own system. What matters is that there should be a clear policy and statement of aims and objectives. That this is by no means to be taken for granted is evident from the results of the 1987 survey of careers work undertaken for the National Association of Careers and Guidance Teachers by David Cleaton. Cleaton found that only four out of five schools provided careers education to third-year and sixth-form pupils and two out of three gave fourth-year pupils less than half a lesson a week. A quarter of the thousand schools responding to the survey had no written policy for careers and only half of the LEAs had one. There is still a long way to go.

The special needs of sixth-formers

Sixteen-year-old boys and girls have to make mutually exclusive decisions: to remain at school for one or two years, to transfer to a college of further education or to chance their luck in the world of employment/ YTS/ unemployment. They are inevitably conditioned by their previous education and the guidance they may have received along the way. The choice of secondary school at eleven, twelve or thirteen will have affected some succeeding choices and opportunities because some schools offer courses and subjects not available in others and all have particular approaches to the curriculum which may affect pupils' ultimate choice of continued education or career. Some schools are demonstrably more examination orientated than others, some are relatively isolated, while others have close contacts with the local community, and each varies in its links with further education, employment and the youth and community services.

The connection between subjects, such as mathematics, physics and technology, is as important as the absolute choices across the whole spectrum of options. The width or narrowness of the core curriculum affects the base on which decisions at sixteen may be made; if physical science is compulsory to the age of sixteen it will ensure a wider choice of career than if it is included in the options and can be eliminated by those youngsters not originally attracted to it. Dropping a foreign language may affect the choice of university later on. Those advising pupils and students over the age of sixteen are, therefore, presented with a range of background experience which will affect the later options available – a particular problem for teachers in LEAs providing schools for the eleven to sixteen age range, followed by tertiary colleges.

School sixth forms usually contain three groups of pupils who have differing guidance needs. Those on one-year courses of general education may lead to retakes or additional passes in GCSE or a CPVE with some mildly vocational content. Some programmes are frankly remedial, others quasi-vocational and may involve links with other schools in a consortium or with a local college. Some are designed deliberately as a bridge towards further education especially for those pupils who may appear to be somewhat disenchanted with school, but could be motivated to greater effort by contact with the more adult atmosphere of a college. Some may have had a taste of work-related activities on a TVEI programme and wish to consolidate it by prevocational education to give them a better chance of a job and training. Many of these sixth-formers may feel they no longer need any careers education or guidance; others could clearly do with an extension of the programme provided in the main school years.

The second group of students are those taking one-year vocational courses for a business or secretarial career, catering, pre-nursing and other work-related programmes. They may have fairly limited needs for careers guidance if they had sound advice before embarking upon the course and the local employment market is favourable.

The third group may appear to present few guidance problems if they are on traditional two-year courses leading to 'A' level or Scottish Highers and aiming at university entrance. Teachers are familiar with this route, but in many cases the subjects chosen at sixteen do not fit the requirements of a later choice of course or career and these pupils may need considerable careers and educational counselling. Subject teachers are often most influential on their plans for higher education and subsequent employment. Headteachers will find it economical and effective to provide a course within the general studies part of the timetable to enable the sixth-form or careers tutors to deal with such topics as university entry, polytechnic entry, college of higher education courses, other forms of full-time post-school course, employment after 'A' levels and financial matters. Students profit by open discussion of subjects and courses, institutions and locations, graduate careers and second chances for those who drop off the academic escalator. Many sixth-formers think they have made a firm and reasoned decision on the next stage only to find in classroom discussion that other ideas might be worth investigating. Opportunity for such discussion should lessen the complaint often heard from undergraduates that they were never told at school about courses not directly in line with the subjects they were studying at school. The head of careers may devise curricular modules appropriate for the whole range of academic ability within the sixth form in order to combat any tendency towards the formation of an academic elite, but some topics are clearly best treated in small, selective groups, preferably by self-selection of interested students even if inappropriate to their abilities.

Tutors and advisers may be reminded that fifth-form pupils should have information on alternatives to the sixth form; some of the academically able may be better off in a college offering subjects not available at school while some of the scholastically weaker youngsters may flourish in a college where the flexibility of programmes enables them to undertake new forms of experiential learning which the school does not wish to provide. Finally, teachers should ensure that youngsters at risk of unemployment are aware of the help which may be available from specialist careers and youth officers. These specialists may be able to attract them to short courses of social and careers education through the youth and community service.

Chapter 6
Resources for Careers Education and Guidance

Teachers

Headteachers who have not been convinced of the necessity to provide adequate resources to careers education should note that Her Majesty's Inspectors are displaying considerable interest and concern in this area and are likely to include reference to it in reports on their visits and inspections. The Secretaries of State for England, Wales and Employment have demanded high level attention from local education authorities to careers education and guidance, so it is likely that this somewhat Cinderella area of the curriculum will receive increasing attention in future. Headteachers must ensure that they make suitable provision for it in their allocation of scarce resources.

The first and most important resource is, of course, the team of teachers covering the subject; their selection and work are described in the next chapter.

Physical resources

There must be some place in the school, clearly identified and centrally situated, where pupils and parents can have access to the wealth of information about courses and occupations. Books and pamphlets should not be locked in the careers teachers' room or scattered irretrievably amongst the general material in the library. They should be housed in a specific section of the main library, under the control of the librarian, or, more effectively, in a resource area where they can be studied and borrowed easily. Access to a computer terminal and hardware for visual aids is invaluable.

There ought to be a classroom for the teaching of careers – probably not for the exclusive use of careers teachers in a small school, but where the displays on the walls belong to the subject and there are adequate cupboards for storing pupils' materials and workbooks. This classroom should have sockets for TV and micros and all walls provided with pegboards for notices and posters.

Some part of the main corridors or foyers of the school should be set aside for the display of careers information and wallcharts and known to be the place to look for a calendar of activities arranged by the careers department.

There must be an office for the use of careers teachers and careers officers which is sealed (not open to eavesdropping from outside), equipped with comfortable chairs, a desk, filing cabinet, noticeboard, typewriter, telephone and micro. It is impossible for careers advisers to give confidential interviews to pupils and parents if they do not have proper provision and, in my view, it is not sufficient for them to be allowed the use of one of the general interviewing rooms provided for pastoral staff. There should be a proper careers office in every school where the teachers can keep their reference and confidential material.

Finance

The careers department needs specific funds for books, stationery, video and radio tapes and disbursements for pupil activities outside school. Experience and observation suggest that 1 per cent of the total sum allocated departmentally each year is the minimum for an adequate careers programme and library.

Time for careers

There has never been any attempt to lay down a standard for the amount of teacher or pupil time required for careers work. Numerous models exist. A minimum provision should ensure coverage of the most important topics in a developmental guidance programme and allow sufficient flexibility to take account of pupils' interests. It should include experiential learning as well as traditional classroom study by lecture, discussion, reading, audio-visual aids and written exercises. As an example one can consider an imaginary school of six-form entry with about a third of the pupils staying in the sixth form. If careers has been timetabled for 2·5 per cent of the pupils' time in the three main school years several strategies can be employed to achieve that quantity of pupils' exposure to formal careers education. It may require the flexibility of blocks of time, intensive courses after the summer examinations or double and triple periods alternating with other subjects. But the goal of 2·5 per cent of pupils' time for three years should be kept in sight; it will enable them, for example, to enter the JIIG-CAL computerised guidance system satisfactorily.

Teachers' time is harder to calculate because it depends on the extent to which the careers team is responsible for tasks other than the classroom teaching of careers. Do they, for instance, draft references and testimonials for leavers or keep detailed records of pupils' curricula, examination entries and results, interviews and changing aspirations, or is this done by pastoral staff or the school office? How extensively does the programme of activities involve extra-mural organisations and people? Is written work set and marked? How much does the department depend upon making its own materials to save central funds or is it able to spend generously on published textbooks, workbooks and visual aids? Can it buy computer materials and tapes? How much time do the teachers have to spend seeing films or television programmes before recording them or is there a resources officer to do this automatically in order to build up a bank of material? Is the careers department responsible for work experience and shadowing schemes, link courses with colleges, consortium arrangements, school–industry projects and other new learning experiences? Most important, does the careers department cover sixth-form guidance or is this the sole prerogative of the head of sixth who may jealously guard his or her knowledge of university entry and alternative opportunities for higher education. The headteacher must decide the division of responsibility.

Taking the model of a six-form entry comprehensive school, the careers department should have the equivalent of one full-time teacher according to the following calculation based upon a forty-period week:

One weekly timetabled period for six third, fourth and fifth forms: eighteen periods

Individual interviews with fourth and fifth-year pupils at two per period: two periods

Normal free periods for preparation, marking and cover: eight periods

Administration of careers resource centre, filing, replacement and retrieval of information, record keeping, writing: three periods

Daily period for casual interviews with parents,   five periods
pupils and colleagues, updating teachers' know-
ledge, liaison with careers officers:

Careers input to the sixth form: four periods

By this calculation a twelve-form entry school would require two full-time or four half-time careers teachers and a three-form entry school at least a half-time teacher for careers work up to the statutory school-leaving age with little over for the sixth form.

In schools where this provision of teacher time is divided among several members of staff it is vital that the head of department has sufficient time for the administrative tasks implicit in the organisation of the programme of activities and liaison with the careers officers. Only one period a day has been allocated for counselling because I do not believe that headteachers should regard the careers teachers as counsellors removed from the daily contact with pupils in formal classes. The staff generally must recognise that a proper programme of activities requires time for its organisation. This model does not include time for organising work experience because that requires up to a third of a teacher's time for each class of thirty pupils if there is to be proper preparation, briefing, supervision and follow-up. It is best achieved by allocating a team of teachers to this function for that part of the year when it is in operation. If it is undertaken by the careers department, additional teacher time must be provided as will be required if the school has extensive TVEI schemes involving consultation with the careers teachers.

Colleges of Further Education

Local colleges increasingly provide resources in the form of link courses to give school pupils the opportunity to try their hand at machines, materials and processes which could not be provided in individual schools. Many offer special transition courses for underachieving pupils who may be woefully diffident about their ability to stand on their own feet in the world of industry and commerce. Some work-experience schemes have only been made possible by the cooperation of colleges because present conditions make it harder for teachers to persuade employers to provide the necessary facilities. Sixth-formers can visit colleges of higher education and universities, sometimes spending a day or more in different departments, sampling halls of residence and attending lectures with students. This is a most valuable experience in itself apart from its obvious usefulness in helping them to make realistic applications for places in higher education.

The Careers Service

The most important resource external to the school is the local Careers Service. Teachers no longer expect careers officers to teach classes on a regular basis as they have more urgent claims on their time as a result of youth unemployment. Careers officers are not usually teacher-trained, but have been specifically trained in interviewing techniques and the principles of vocational guidance on their post-graduate courses. They have a detailed knowledge of the requirements of courses in universities, polytechnics, colleges of all kinds and of employment opportunities locally, regionally and nationally, besides forming the main link between the schools and the YTS programme of the Manpower Services Commission. Because they are not teachers with a timetable of classes to take they have better opportunities than teachers to visit a wide range of employers to discuss training provisions and to stimulate openings for young people.

Support staff

Clerical help is now often provided for careers teachers; this may be an allocation of so many hours a week from the total school allowance of office staff, realistic work done by pupils studying office skills in a department of business studies or volunteer help from parents or friends of the school. No programme of extra-mural activities of the complexity desirable in a good careers programme can operate without proper correspondence, records and filing. It is useful for the careers officer to have duplicate keys for the cabinet containing records of the pupils in case he or she needs information during school holidays when teachers are absent but some pupils need urgent interviews.

Other human resources

Among the other resources sometimes neglected by those given responsibility for careers guidance are other teachers in the school who may have forged connections with local employers and colleges in order to enrich the work done in their subject by, for instance, visits to bakeries, building sites or factories. Those headteachers who have adopted the concept of community schools have often acquired many contacts in the local community and in some cases formed twinning arrangements with nearby industrial or commercial firms. Visitors from the associated enterprises may take part in activities for teachers and pupils, provide classroom materials or ideas for scientific experiments which the pupils can carry out in the laboratories as realistic problem-solving exercises.

Other employees of the LEA include educational psychologists and youth officers as well as tutors in adult education institutes who may represent a number of interesting occupations in their main work. Parents are a rich source of people to take part in careers conventions and symposia to give present pupils the chance to find out more about the working world than they can acquire from formal visits to workplaces, reading or watching videos. Past pupils are often flattered to be asked to come to school to meet pupils interested to hear about their experiences in looking for work or coping with unemployment. Pupils' own experience of holiday and weekend work is seldom utilised, but can make an effective contribution to classroom discussion of careers. Many social services, church-related agencies and community centres arrange conferences for school-leavers. Local Rotary clubs and branches of the Soroptimists or Business and Professional Women's clubs show goodwill towards a careers teacher who approaches them for contacts or ideas. Employers' associations and trades unions frequently help with careers exhibitions and conventions or suggest members who might speak to groups of pupils. They may also give individual advice to a youngster who may be on the brink of making a firm career choice, but would benefit from discussion with a knowledgeable outsider.

Headteachers keen to involve adults other than teachers in the education of their pupils have to make sometimes difficult policy decisions because there is obviously a limit to the amount of time which can reasonably be spent on these activities. Parents have been known to complain if their children's education appears to be suffering in preparation for examinations by the quantity of such non-examination learning. Sensitive use of local contacts must be an enrichment of the total curriculum, however, and excellent work has been seen in the follow-up to visits and lectures of this kind. General studies for sixth-formers or social education classes of younger pupils have enjoyed discussions on aspects of the adult world using these external resources to deal with topics such as company structures and hierarchies; the role of management; labour relations; the function of trades unions and professional bodies; the progress by which raw materials become finished goods; financing trade and industry; market research and expansion; diversification and changing consumer demand. All these valuable aspects of general education can be undertaken at little cost beyond the initial approaches and research into local resources, and the careers officer should be able to produce invaluable contacts.

The local council is often the largest employer in the community and can provide many resources to teachers of economics, history, science, social studies and careers in the way of maps of the area, copies of historical documents, statistics of population, movement of industry and commerce into and out of the district, the financing of local services and so forth. Local government employs four hundred identifiable occupations and it can be an instructive exercise to get pupils to find out how many are represented in the local town hall or council office.

School pupils are sometimes encountered in the street conducting a survey of passers-by as part of a general studies class; a survey of job satisfactions and frustrations can easily be undertaken without venturing beyond the school gates if one lists the many jobs featured on school premises. If pupils design a questionnaire and conduct interviews (preferably by tape recorder to increase communication skills) and retain the material for future classroom use, they can learn much about the motivation, training, rewards, successes, irritations and disappointments inherent in people's working lives.

Among people normally working at the school are:
Teachers, including the head and deputy and perhaps some who had
   other careers before entering teaching;
Administrative officer or bursar;
Secretary, clerks and typists;
Caretaker;
Groundsman and gardener;
Librarian;
Laboratory technician;
Media resources officer, ETV or AVA technician;
School nurse;
Meals supervisor, cooks and kitchen assisstants;
Cleaners.

A second group represents people who are not on school premises every day, but may be easily found on occasions:

Doctor and dentist with surgery assistant;
Social worker/educational welfare officer;
Careers officer;
Part-time teachers of instrumental music, sports and games;
Coach and bus driver;
Postman;
Milkman and other delivery persons with stationery or supplies;
Administrative officers from the LEA;
HM Inspectors of Schools;
LEA Inspectors and Advisers.

There are also people who may visit the school occasionally:

Governors and Education Committee members representing many
  careers;
Youth leaders and youth officers;
Clergy and other ministers of religion;
Police officers;
Fire Service officers;
Safety officers;
Probation officers;
Social workers from the LEA, voluntary agencies such as NSPCC;
Piano tuners;
Window cleaners;
Heating, ventilating and building services technicians;
Typewriter mechanics;
Building tradesmen, plumbers, carpenters, bricklayers, electricians,
  glaziers, painters and decorators.
Refuse collectors.

Chapter 7

Specialist Careers and Guidance Teachers

If careers is regarded as a subject and timetabled it is important for everyone in the school to know who is responsible for it. In all but the smallest secondary schools it is best if there is a team of teachers, preferably drawn from different subject departments and led by a head of a department with status equivalent to the head of history or geography. Inspectors and advisers are sometimes asked to suggest a different title for this staff member and in some schools the person responsible for careers is called 'careers counsellor', 'careers tutor', 'careers coordinator' or 'vocational counsellor'. While accepting the arguments for using a title to reflect the varying concept of that person's role, I prefer the term 'careers teacher', in order to make clear the distinction between a teacher and the careers officer and to stress that this teacher is expected to teach classes regularly. The Scottish term 'guidance teacher' has merit, but can be confused with the staff of the child guidance unit dealing with learning problems. The double title used by the professional association is entirely acceptable, but somewhat clumsy. So 'careers teacher' it shall be in this book.

Whatever the title, careers teachers are now accepted as a necessary part of the academic and pastoral structure of any secondary school. Regrettably, though, many of them still have limited resources of time, finance, accommodation, equipment and status.

The team

A team of teachers for careers education has clear advantages over the appointment of a single-handed practitioner. It enables some specialisation of role and function, either into arts and sciences for careers information specialisation, or between those most concerned for the less academically successful and younger leavers and those more attuned to the interests of potential sixth-formers and undergraduates. Some heads of careers undertake all the administrative arrangements themselves and leave most of the classroom teaching to colleagues in the team.

Where there are several teachers in the careers team their timetables can be so arranged as to provide for team teaching, so that large groups can be assembled in the hall for a film or lecture and then broken up into small groups for follow-up or project work. School governors occasionally demand that all schools should have a full-time careers teacher, but the arguments for a team of part-time careers teachers are compelling, provided the head of department has the necessary status and stature within the staffroom to perform that function successfully and obtain the cooperation of other colleagues. Any subject involving varied activities, many outside the school, is bound to need sensitive treatment to avoid upsetting other teachers who dislike individual pupils missing their classes or being asked to change rooms in order that a group may use a computer or television or work with maps and plans.

In a few schools the deputy head is responsible for careers, or the job is given to a senior teacher to combine with that of director of studies, curriculum coordinator or examinations coordinator. In a number of instances careers responsibility is attached to a year head for fourth or fifth years or to the head of sixth form or of upper school. That is a matter for decision within each school. High status in the school hierarchy has some obvious advantages, but may make the office holder remote from the pupils and less able to deal with individual problems or give clear leadership to the subject team.

According to David Cleaton's 1987 survey 83 per cent of senior careers teachers were regarded as heads of department, so that seems to be the most generally accepted position. Given the status of a departmental head, to whom is the careers teacher accountable? It is usually advisable for that person to be directly responsible to the headteacher or one of the deputies, but it must be clearly established that the head of careers has functions and responsibilities in both the pastoral and academic life of the school. He or she should automatically be a member of the academic board or coordinating committee for curriculum matters, but should also attend meetings of pastoral heads. One of the most challenging functions of a head of careers is in staff training and awareness of factors affecting the school from the local economy and community.

The head of careers can reasonably be required to report on the careers activities and employment situation for leavers at meetings of the governing body. He or she should have a well-established system for communication with staffroom colleagues so that careers work is seen as cross-curricular and all resources are used to further it.

If the school is on several sites one member of the team should be teaching in each building in which there are pupils from the third year. It sometimes happens that all the careers teachers work in the upper school, thereby denying the younger boys and girls the chance of casual contact which can often be influential on their perceptions of occupations and their own future. At thirteen they must consider the careers consequences of their option choices and this is facilitated if one of the careers teachers is regularly in their building and has some resources there to answer their questions. If there is only one careers teacher it is important that he or she does not concentrate only on pupils in the upper school.

The qualities required

What sort of people make good careers teachers? There is no recipe, and examples of effective members of careers teams can be found with many different abilities and backgrounds. Some have had Ph.Ds and others only one year of emergency training – with every variant of qualification in between. Excellent careers teachers have come out of every subject stable and it is not necessary that they should be teachers of supposedly vocational subjects such as technology or business studies. Nor is it always an advantage for a careers teacher to have entered teaching after trying other careers first. They sometimes exhibit fierce prejudices against the sector of industry or commerce in which they were themselves unsuccessful or unhappy. Obviously they have good inside knowledge of the structure of an enterprise and can be effective in countering the accusation of parents that teachers do not understand the problems faced by workers in industry, commerce and the professions. But it is not a *sine qua non* for a careers teacher to have worked outside teaching first. Headteachers asking for volunteers to join the careers team have sometimes been surprised at the apparently unlikely people responding. Sometimes a teacher is attracted to careers work just because he or she has no knowledge of the world outside teaching and wants the chance to see something of it. In other cases the motivation is simpler in that there appears to be no promotion within their original subject department and increased job satisfaction may accrue from some change of role. Some of the most effective careers teachers have orginally taught physical education and find they cannot face a lifetime of blowing whistles on chilly games fields!

Qualities of personality and temperament are most significant. Headteachers should look for evidence of an unprejudiced attitude towards work at all levels, sympathetic understanding of the predicament of leavers for whom there may be no work available and a good grasp of economic facts and forces which determine employment opportunities. Intellectual curiosity about other people's work and lifestyles is paramount and should be backed by sufficient mental energy to absorb a mass of knowledge about the requirements of courses and careers in order to answer the pupils' questions and help colleagues to see the relationship of their subject specialisms to the demands of occupations.

Careers teachers must be prepared to spend time with parents who may be difficult or diffident and exhibit a genuine interest in the problems of teenagers as they grow through adolescence into stable adulthood. Lastly, careers is no haven for unhappy teachers who cannot interest a class in their subject. It requires exciting presentation of unfamiliar material and the readiness to try out new methods of experiential learning besides all the normal weapons in teachers' armoury. No other subject offers such a variety of material, method and process, nor so many contacts outside the school. It can offer professional fulfilment to teachers of all intellectual, practical and social interests and make use of all sorts of capacities and characteristics.

Responsibilities

Headteachers and senior colleagues may not always be clear on the responsibilities of a head of department of careers and guidance whose work is made more difficult just because the teachers in the department may have very varied backgrounds. The prime task is the organisation of a programme of careers work throughout the year, involving many colleagues and all main school pupils. Establishing curricular modules for each group of pupils, allocating tasks and distributing material to tutors and other colleagues is additional to the normal administration of a team of teachers in a department. Working with the careers officer, a schedule will be publicised for pupils to be interviewed. The collation of assessments of performance and potential on which the careers officer will base advice and guidance will already have been arranged with colleagues. The year's programme of events is unlikely to follow the previous year's exactly and there will need to be endless contingency plans to guard against sudden changes occasioned by the unavailability of some extra-mural resource. Constant communication with the headteacher and other colleagues will ensure the smoothest running of the various ingredients in the calendar of events.

One of the team will need to be charged with custody of the careers education resource centre and the information in the library by removing out-of-date literature, ordering new material and checking the condition of posters and wallcharts on display. Someone must order the annual reference books, directories and prospectuses so that the main information bank is up-to-date and additional copies are available for colleagues undertaking guidance functions. The head of department will normally take on the liaison with further education colleges and the careers officers. He or she will also monitor the schemes of work proposed by each member of the team in order to ensure that all groups of pupils have the basic careers education programme and that the teachers have access to all the appropriate materials. Naturally that includes some qualitative assessment of the work done by pupils by regular inspection of workbooks and folders. Colleagues in other departments may have to be consulted as to their contribution to the total programme and information distributed in the staffroom whenever some event is planned which may interest other teachers' pupils or involve groups of pupils being out of school or a parents' meeting on careers.

Constant review of pupils' records will ensure that they are kept up-to-date and consultation with tutors will help prevent some of the communication breakdowns which occur from time to time otherwise. If all pupils are interviewed annually from the fourth year a rota will have to be worked out and information passed to and from tutors and careers teachers with more information if anything significant transpires at a pupil's interview with a careers officer. All members of the careers team should visit the careers office at least once a year to get the latest news of training and employment while as many as possible in the team should be encouraged to attend meetings of the local careers association if one exists.

The head of department may delegate to one of the team the detailed organisation of such events as a careers convention, exhibition of local industries or higher education, but the head of department will be held accountable if anything goes wrong and must take overall responsibility. There may also be special leavers' days or joint events with other schools in a consortium or a local college. Delegation can enhance the job satisfaction of members of the team in other ways. The programme of visits for pupils to see workplaces may involve other heads of departments who may be arranging visits themselves in connection with their subject and welcome collaboration. A programme of talks on careers or a week or fortnight of talks and demonstrations can be arranged by another teacher, but the head of department will need to discuss with the headteacher for which groups of pupils these events are to be provided. They should also consider whether a whole class or year are to attend, with the risk of boredom or misbehaviour by some, or whether only keen volunteers are to attend, with the concomitant risk of an insufficient audience for a good or important speaker.

In some schools the responsibility for administration of interest inventories or the programme of computerised guidance is devolved on to a young and enthusiastic careers teacher with only minimal supervision by the head of department. Cumulative record keeping in the careers department is often an indication that those teachers are responsible for drafting the references and testimonials for leavers. Examination results usually come out during the summer holidays and some heads of careers arrange to be present in school during results week so that they can help any pupils whose results are better or worse than expected and which may affect their future plans.

Some heads of careers are responsible for the careers guidance of sixth-form pupils. Where the head of the sixth year may also give advice both teachers must ensure proper coordination so that advice is continuous and there is no possibility of conflicting information. Any scheme of work experience or shadowing is likely to involve the careers department even if another teacher is responsible for its organisation. It is unthinkable that a year head or social studies teacher asked to arrange work experience would do so without collaborating with the head of careers, whose knowledge and contacts would be invaluable and whose position at the centre of the school's curriculum and activities should be apparent from the range of tasks described.

Training

Like other heads of department the head of careers is responsible for training colleagues joining the department from elsewhere in the school or on appointment from outside. This task is particularly onerous because most newcomers to careers education have had no training in the subject as it hardly ever figures in a PGCE or B.Ed. course. It may be difficult for the newcomer to find time to do the necessary reading and enquiry when he or she already has a commitment to another department with its own demands.

It is often preferable for teachers to get some experience in a careers department before enrolling on one of the part-time courses offered by some colleges and polytechnics to enable teachers to obtain an advanced diploma in careers education and guidance. In this way they can be sure they will like the work before committing themselves to the very considerable effort involved in taking a course which is likely to involve an evening a week for two years. Courses in universities and polytechnics for a post-graduate diploma on a full-time basis have not increased demonstrably because so few teachers have been able to get release for a year's full-time study; in David Cleaton's survey only 4 per cent of the respondents had obtained a qualification in this way. The part-time courses have proved popular and successful as they enable the teachers to integrate their theoretical study with practical experience in a careers department. Headteachers and school governors should support any application from a suitable teacher who asks for remission of a period or two a week in order to travel to the course or for a grant towards the fees, travelling expenses and books. A teacher needs encouragement to undertake a course which is not a requirement but is undoubtedly valuable, not only in carrying out the careers work more effectively, but in commending the holder of a specific qualification in careers for subsequent promotion. Only by demonstrating that careers is a specialist educational field for which there is proper post-graduate training will the subject acquire the same status as other new areas of the curriculum.

Chapter 8

Careers and the Rest of the School

The isolated careers teacher

Careers education and guidance is so important to the pupils and so integral to the process of secondary education that some newly appointed careers teachers find the responsibility daunting. In schools where there may be only one designated careers teacher or a head of department with part-time help from one other teacher, it is also very isolating. A powerful argument for releasing careers teachers to attend meetings of local careers associations stems from their need to overcome the loneliness of their position. There are, of course, other teachers of minority subjects who are similarly placed, but at least they have confidence from possessing a qualification in the subject whereas opportunities for training in careers work are usually limited to in-service courses.

In order to overcome some careers teachers' isolation and fear of overweening responsibility a headteacher can encourage diffusion of some of the total careers programme by establishing clear guidelines of responsibility. He or she should also ensure by personal attention that proper provision is achieved under a head of careers capable of the necessary coordination. There are various methods: setting up departmental information banks, using tutorial time, extra-mural resources and infusion through the curriculum of other subjects. But it can never be a substitute for, rather a supplement to, identifiable and regular time-tabled careers education taught by a keen and specially trained teacher who can coordinate these elements undertaken by colleagues into an integrated and developing programme.

Classrooms

As classrooms, laboratories, workshops and gymnasia are normally associated with the teaching of a particular subject or subjects, they should have a noticeboard or resource corner containing material on all those careers which have some connection with that subject. The occupational literature distributed to schools can be dispersed accordingly (if spare copies are obtained) in order to reinforce the well-known fact that young people are often more influenced by the teacher of their best or favourite subject than they are by the formal guidance apparatus of the school carried out by form tutors, careers teachers and careers officers. Pupils' desire to continue an activity enjoyed at school, whether a language, science, humanity, practical or aesthetic subject, may well be motivated to do better if they can see a vocational connection. Obviously one must beware of undue emphasis on the occupational utility of most school subjects because it may be comparatively tenuous and lead to heightened frustration when no apparently suitable job is forthcoming at the school-leaving stage. It needs to be recognised, however.

Subject teachers

As a first step, subject teachers in traditional departments might take an interest in courses of higher and further education which have some connection with their subject and acquire some basic knowledge of the possible subsequent careers. This will help to diffuse some of the information and guidance which might otherwise fall only upon teachers in the careers department and will complement the work of the sixth-form tutor.

With falling rolls many teachers are considering taking on additional responsibilities in order to protect their own careers and promote a broad curriculum for the pupils. Since teachers do not normally enter the profession equipped to undertake careers work, this is an area which can be taken up by teachers regardless of their initial subject discipline. So a headteacher may encourage a colleague whose main subject is perhaps one not chosen by many pupils to undertake some careers education as a second string.

In many schools the head of careers expects some colleagues to take on aspects of the programme of careers education if he or she has other responsibilities or spends considerable time teaching another subject. The use of form tutor time for much of the careers work presupposes an energetic head of careers who can equip the tutors with materials and resources which they in turn may welcome to fill form periods productively. Beyond that, there are areas of a careers education syllabus which can be effectively taught within main subject departments provided there is time apart from the demands of examinations and the head of careers ensures that every pupil covers the essential topics and gets appropriate experience of decision taking, problem solving, self-assessment and adequate background knowledge to make a reasonable choice of career. The following suggestions illustrate contributions which other teachers might be expected to make to the total coverage arranged by the careers department.

The *English* department can be asked to tackle letters of application for jobs, application forms, writing references or testimonials for a friend; study of newspaper advertisements for jobs of all levels and skills; analysis of notices, instructions and handbooks which pupils have collected or copied from visits to industry to assess comprehension; tape-recording interviews with workers to discuss job satisfaction and frustration; autobiographies and biographies or novels which provide background information on work and lifestyles; essays on work, descriptions of careers activities, imaginary obituaries and autobiographies; and correspondence relating to careers activities.

Speech and *Drama* teachers frequently arrange practice in interview techniques for young school-leavers going to workplaces or sixth-formers taking university or college entrance; using the telephone is a useful skill and study of television plays can be illuminating in their portrayal of work in current or historical settings.

Mathematics classes regularly tackle exercises on personal budgeting, comparative wages, taxation, insurance, saving, hire purchase and social security benefits. Material can be obtained by judicious contact with local firms to give pupils practice in problem solving in addition to the computational skills still demanded in many jobs. Some employers have given pupils real problems which they have not been able to solve and actual examples of the need for accurate measurement which youngsters do not always appreciate. Statistics on aspects of the national economy, movement of industry, employment and unemployment can be culled from newspapers and journals; figures of university entry degree classes and graduate employment are readily available. Mini-enterprises, business games and simulations have a considerable mathematical content and provide practice in calculation, problem solving and decision taking as well as insight into the work of industrial managers. Much stimulus and help will accrue if mathematics teachers can join a local branch of Mathematics for Education and Industry (MEI).

Science teachers are in a strong position to enthuse pupils with the vocational relevance of their subject and encourage more sixth-formers to apply for degree courses in applied science and engineering – for which there is still a shortage of able applicants and a wide choice of graduate careers. The history of scientific discoveries, the relationship of technology to science, the exploitation of scientific and technological innovation, and lives of scientists and engineers are all career-related topics. Technology in the home may interest girls for whom industry has no appeal. Several companies in science-based industries have produced resources to enrich science curricula through the Association for Science Education. Physics and chemistry are the most vocationally useful subjects taken in public examinations, but biology can have a strong thread of careers content if it includes sex and health education, physiology and elementary psychology in which pupils discuss human differences, aptitudes and abilities in relation to the requirements of occupations.

Computer studies may be timetabled and taught by a specialist whose work can assist the careers department by help with programs on career choice and job information. Discussion of the implications of industrial and commercial computerisation on employment and training is also useful. Hands-on experience with computers and the acquisition of keyboard skills should be compulsory for all pupils and can be achieved in a concentrated course during the early years of secondary schooling, if it has not been accomplished during the primary school years.

History, Geography, Social studies and Religious Education deal with the importance of work in people's lives, now and in the past. By discussing the historical background to the area, identifying predominant industries established since the industrial revolution and geographical factors affecting the local economy, they can map significant points affecting the location of industry and commerce, movement of population, goods and services, transport policies, availability of raw materials, and issues of conservation and energy supplies as they affect the environment. These subjects also include the functions of trade unions and professional bodies, the relationship between central and local government, implications of unemployment, division of labour, integration of working life and social life and government policies on import and export of goods and services. They alert pupils to the impact of designated development area status skill demarcation, the dangers of sex and race stereotyping, and the influence of multi-national companies and international trade. Further work can deal with welfare rights and voluntary social work, study of a company to analyse its occupational structure, recruitment, education and training of the workforce, job satisfaction, prospects and rewards, and the work-ethic in a society where miro-electronics may render it no longer tenable according to a survey conducted on future job opportunities.

Economics and *Business studies* have obvious relevance to the future employment of pupils in the class with a special interest in these subjects and to others who may be taking them but proposing to enter unrelated careers such as music or nursing. Basic economic literacy should be a universal acquisition in order that young people understand the background to their working and family lives and role as citizens. Business studies has for so long been regarded as primarily vocational that it is hard to persuade parents that all boys and girls should be competent in office skills such as filing and keyboarding. Business studies departments sometimes give pupils realistic experience by servicing the careers department with library monitors, filing clerks, correspondence writers and record keepers. They can also undertake interesting surveys of the destiny of past pupils, examination results, job advertisements in local and national newspapers, tasks done by people on school premises and analyses of comparative rewards and conditions. These exercises reinforce theoretical instruction on principles of statistics and interpretation of data in graph and diagram form. All contribute to pupils' understanding of the commercial world.

Home economics, cookery, health care and nutrition should be part of the preparation of all young people for adult life. For some this may mean a career as a nutritionist, food scientist or hotel manager, but for all it will give confidence if they are shortly to face the uncertainties of moving away from home in pursuit of a job or training. All pupils benefit from classes designed to help them to acquire social skills, talk to strangers, order meals in a restaurant, and appreciate consumer protection and advertising practice, besides basic cooking, needlework and personal budgeting. Careers teachers welcome help from home economists in preparing pupils for presenting themselves at interviews and in discussions of the role of women in employment, dual career families and the responsibility of both parents in bringing up children and home maintenance.

Craft, Design and Technology used to be regarded primarily as preparation for boys intending to enter skilled manual jobs, but it has changed dramatically in recent years so that it now provides excellent opportunities for girls and boys to practise problem solving, apply mathematics and science to practical tasks, understand graphs, plans and diagrams, appreciate the significance of technology in the home and office as well as industryy, and counteract the anti-technology attitudes of some of those who are specialising in humanities and languages. CDT teachers can be influential in persuading more academically able youngsters to aspire to careers in engineering and industrial design by demonstrating its importance to the national economy and built environment.

Modern and *Classical Languages* have apparently least connection with careers, despite the implications of membership of the Common Market and increase in travel and tourism. Mutual recognition of qualifications should be discussed when pupils are thinking about future qualifications and training. Language teachers can devise interesting projects for pupils to collect foreign newspapers and magazines and compare the reports of changing industries or job advertisements with those found in British papers, besides studying the careers which give opportunities for using less common languages in work and for long or short periods of overseas residence. Those studying non-European languages or from a family background in African, Asian or Oriental languages may discuss concepts of lifestyles and working patterns in unfamiliar climates and societies to further the school's multi-cultural policies. Classicists can be encouraged by studying the correlation of their subject with success in computer programming, analysing the reasons.

Art, Drama, Music and *Dance* departments are the obvious means whereby pupils with appropriate talents and interests get ideas and information about possible careers in those fields. Drama teachers are particularly helpful to the careers department in concocting role-playing situations relevant to careers education, such as discussions between parents and children, managers and workers, industrial relations, trade union concerns and job loss or redundancy. Some art departments have produced delightful displays of drawings and paintings on the theme of work which can enliven the corridors by the careers rooms when no longer wanted in the art studio.

Physical Education teachers may welcome ideas for classroom work when they cannot use gyms or playing fields. These can usefully supplement work done in careers on the physical demands and requirements of jobs, relevance of good health and fitness to job satisfaction and success, or study of careers which may not be available to leavers with certain physical handicaps or limitations. Residential experience is valuable in developing self-confidence; it can be especially useful if teachers can devise activities which simulate the rhythm of the industrial day which is often so much less physically active and varied than the school day. With greater emphasis on individual activities in place of team games, PE departments can contribute notably to developing self-confidence, which is perhaps the most important facet of a school's efforts to prepare leavers for employment.

Work Experience

Teachers from any department may be asked to organise a scheme of work experience, observation, sampling or shadowing. Such activities are sometimes attached to a department of *Social and Personal Development* on the grounds that it has most to offer to those boys and girls who have dropped many of the traditional academic subjects and have time for extra-mural components in a less intellectually demanding learning programme. It should be recognised, however, that work experience is valuable for all pupils regardless of their academic potential or career plans. Careers teachers should reiterate at staff meetings the desirability of other teachers informing them when a party of pupils is to visit a bakery, building site, engineering works or office so that interested individual pupils may be attached to the party to further their career decision taking. Academically able pupils can learn a lot in a one or two-day attachment to shadow a manager or professional practitioner. These activities supplement the formal careers classes and require detailed curriculum planning and openness between colleagues; the head of careers in a large school must be a good organiser and clever manipulator of colleagues!

The pastoral structure

Pastoral care is a term much used, and sometimes misused, in secondary schools; in trying to define it one runs the risk of setting rigid boundaries to an aspect of education which is seminal and integral to the basic concepts of comprehensive education. In this book 'pastoral' is not used in opposition to 'academic', but as its complement. There is a pastoral curriculum comprising parts of the pupils' development of knowledge, skills and attitudes which the academic curriculum purports to achieve through traditional subjects. In Michael Marland's definitive book *Pastoral Care* (Heinemann, 1974) the term embraces 'looking after the total welfare of the pupil' and consists of 'complementary separate aims':
    (i) to assist the individual to enrich his personal life;
    (ii) to help prepare the young person for educational choice;

(iii) to offer guidance or counselling, helping young people to make their own decisions – by question and focus, and by information where appropriate:

(iv) to support the 'subject' teaching;

(v) to assist the individual to develop his or her own lifestyle and to respect that of others;

(vi) to maintain an orderly atmosphere in which all this is possible.

In a contribution to *Perspectives on Pastoral Care* by Best, Jarvis and Ribbins (Heinemann, 1980) the same writer makes the case for the pastoral curriculum as distinct from pastoral care of individual pupils, and defines its purpose as 'to establish the concepts, attitudes, facts and skills which are necessary to the individual' by 'curriculum components which relate especially to individual and personal growth'. In the same book A. G. Watts and Beryl Fawcett consider the role of careers education in these components. I believe the American term 'vocational maturity' can be used to describe the end to which this process is directed and allows all teachers to contribute towards it. Much careers education and guidance can be undertaken as part of the pastoral work of the school, provided the headteacher has ensured that there is proper coordination and underpinning by the specialist careers teachers.

Form tutors

All tutors at some time will be involved in work which could be described as guidance or counselling and in most schools all but the most senior teachers have pastoral responsibility for a group of pupils to whom they are tutor. Most teachers have some contact with parents and there is overlap between careers guidance and the questions sometimes asked by parents which seem simply to relate to their children's academic progress, choice of subjects or dislike of a certain teacher, but where the tutor must be aware of any possible consequences upon career choice. Teachers are sometimes accused of trying to persuade able pupils that their subject is of more utility vocationally than any objective assessment would substantiate. It is not unknown for pupils to claim that they were overpersuaded at the stage of choosing 'A' levels and that they should have had more objective advice from a careers adviser or less involved head of year or house.

Some schools set up committees and working parties. This can create difficulties for careers teachers who belong to a pastoral team and subject department so cannot have meetings of the careers department at times when they are required to attend meetings of their main department. The situation can occur particularly when careers education is widely diffused among a number of teachers.

When careers teachers themselves undertake pastoral functions as form tutors they may face particular conflict of roles. It is hard for any tutor to discipline a pupil one day for some minor peccadillo and then find that boy or girl requiring advice or counselling on an important decision. Unless the two have a good relationship, the discussion may go by default because the pupil prefers not to consult a teacher whose last contact was in a disciplinary role. Pastoral heads should be alert to these sensitivities.

The social background

The community surrounding the school has obvious relevance for those tutors giving career counselling because the outlook for jobs will vary from place to place and must be taken into account. If, for instance, the school is in a small town or large village where there is very little employment pupils will need extra help to look further afield and contemplate leaving home. Coastal towns where work is mainly seasonal, urban areas with declining industries and some derelict inner city areas present difficulties not faced by tutors in places where there are still job opportunities for a proportion of the leavers. Denominational schools can call upon help from congregations for work experience contacts and possible employment leads.

Schools orientated towards high examination results present tutors with different challenges from those with many disaffected pupils or low achievers who may be inspired to unexpected levels of scholastic success when the careers programme or work experience convinces them of their potential and the need for good results. Many a youngster has been motivated by work experience to a last-minute effort to do better than the teachers predicted.

Ethnic minorities

In schools with large numbers of pupils from ethnic minorities tutors must be ready to prepare them for possible discrimination in employment. The more successful the school has been in implementing a policy of integration in classroom and out-of-school activities, the greater will be the need for tutors to explain to pupils at risk the facts of possible disadvantage later on. Careers officers report that young black school-leavers have to make more applications for jobs than similarly qualified – or unqualified – white youngsters. Equally telling is the experience of some careers teachers who have persuaded black pupils that they can obtain entry to coveted careers or courses if they have the required qualifications. The scarcity of role models of black people in influential positions has to be recognised as a factor by advisers familiar with the comparable problem for able or talented girls; both groups see themselves facing an adult world in which power and influence reside among white males. Relationships between the sexes and generations differ in other cultures and affect the attitudes of parents and pupils towards careers choice, lifestyles and family structures and thus assume importance in guidance. Some teachers advocate special programmes of careers education and guidance for pupils from ethnic minorities. Others believe the total programme should be directed towards integration into the prevailing economy and ethos in order to give all school-leavers equal chances of training for employment and career progress.

Records of past pupils

A particular tutorial function with implications for the careers department is record keeping and contacts with past pupils. Clubs for old boys and old girls are usually associated with sports and fundraising, and are commoner in independent and grammar schools than in ordinary secondary schools despite the proximity of most pupils' homes in comprehensive day schools. If the pastoral system fosters contacts with past pupils, however, the careers department may be able to capitalise on this admirable extension of the pastoral work and use this resource to help the next generation of leavers. This may mean inviting past pupils who are now undergraduates, workers or unemployed to return to school to describe their experiences to present classes or a compilation of a register of those who have taken particular career paths so that present pupils can be put in touch with them for information or given the chance of work experience, shadowing or holiday jobs through their good offices. It is surprising how few schools see their alumni as a valuable resource for the careers department.

Pastoral structures of years or houses

The most obvious way in which the structure of a school affects its careers work is the decision to have a year or house system. In all but the smallest schools there has to be some way for pupils to be allocated to groups with which they can relate more easily than to the whole school. The traditional house system was based upon the boarding house of a public school, where pupils lived for thirteen weeks in a community spanning the age range from eleven or thirteen to eighteen and which provided opportunities for a variety of competitive activities, both sporting and cultural. Houses became common in secondary schools after the Second World War, but headteachers gradually realised that this system did not always provide the experiences which justified the effort put into stimulating house spirit. Year systems seemed more suitable, especially when schools were on split sites. Many have changed from a house system to years, but few reverse the process.

Clearly the careers department must work closely with the heads of house or year as well as tutors with small groups. Some pastoral heads write reports and testimonials. Some interviews with a careers officer are arranged by houses, but most experienced careers advisers prefer to work with a year system because this accords more naturally with their cycle of work.

Within year systems opinions differ on the preference of one teacher keeping the same cohort of pupils from years one to five or for pupils to get to know different pastoral teachers as they move up the school while remaining in their tutorial group of fifteen to twenty. Headteachers, having decided on the amount of non-teaching time to allow tutors and pastoral heads, then have to allocate pupils to groups by ability, primary school, friendships or alphabetically. If the fifth-form tutors change annually the careers advisers have to adjust their arrangements, whereas if the same people have fifth-year responsibilities year after year there is some advantage. If a year head remains with the same cohort from entry to the end of statutory schooling that teacher will only encounter the careers advisers at option choices and when the main careers interviews are scheduled. Whatever system is adopted, senior staff must be aware of the impact of different systems on the work of the careers department and on the opportunities open to pupils for skilled guidance.

Year heads

There are advantages in appointing a particular teacher as head of first year because that individual has an affinity with younger pupils and is successful at induction processes. Another can be kept as head of third year by virtue of expertise over options. Sixth-formers normally have one head of sixth who looks after both year groups and it is logical for fourth and fifth-year pupils to have one year head who can work with them through the two years leading to GCSE. It is especially helpful to the careers officers and other representatives of outside agencies if the same two year heads alternate by having the same group for both years.

Tutors as counsellors

Much of a tutor's work consists in counselling individual boys and girls who manifest or express a need for a chat with a sympathetic adult at some crisis point in their lives. It may be caused by deep personal distress arising from home circumstances, a parent leaving home, sibling committed to prison, death of a grandparent or other domestic crisis. Other youngsters may need counselling because of a learning or social difficulty which makes them unhappy or unsuccessful at school. A boy may not tell anyone that he is being bullied, but a sensitive tutor may discover this by enquiry about the lad's failure to take part in activities with other members of his form, for example. A girl may not be pregnant, but some irregularity in her menstrual cycle, or ignorance through lack of sex education, may lead her to ask questions from which the sensitive tutor deduces that this is the cause of her worries.

The tutor's role in guidance

Some tutors find themselves giving educational and vocational guidance as a concomitant of a request for personal counselling. This is more likely to refer to self-assessment than to the requirements of courses and careers which are properly the concern of careers teachers. Pupils need guidance to appreciate their own strengths and weaknesses, to work through their changing interests and evolve a value system to identify their aspirations and ideals. Tutors may be responsible for setting them interest inventories and simple aptitudes tests; they should certainly keep records of notable changes in educational programme or ambitions. It is helpful for tutors to have information on the requirements of common occupations for examination passes (such as are given in CRAC/Hobsons 'Choice' series of paperbacks), so that they can answer straightforward factual questions which may occur during a tutor period.

Guidance should provide pupils with the necessary skills to plan future courses of action and to have confidence in the services and resources available to them. Individual careers guidance may best be delegated to officers of the Careers Service, but tutors should normally be capable of undertaking much preliminary work in collaboration with the careers teachers who provide the formal careers programme. Tutors exercise a guidance role when pupils enter their form or year group. They must monitor their progress, contact parents, discuss examination entries and interpret the school's policy at appropriate times. Those with fifth-form pupils in their tutor groups need to be alert to the changing employment situation and understand the careers officer's role in introducing leavers to employers and youth training schemes, besides contact with other colleagues on questions of sixth-form subjects or transfer to further education. Some fifth-form tutors arrange for outsiders to conduct mock interviews, preferably in a personnel office or lecturer's study.

Tutors must sometimes consult parents besides informing them of decisions already made about their children's future and from time to time communicate with external agencies such as the police, probation service, education welfare, social services and those voluntary agencies working with young people who have left school. Some schools have tutor-wardens who combine a teaching function in the school with administration of a youth club or centre. Others have members of staff who also teach in adult institutes, thereby enlarging the range of informal contacts to augment the guidance system.

Every school has its own policy on access to pupil records and information on their subsequent education and careers. Many tutors keep in touch with their pupils for many years, thus acquiring considerable knowledge of the problems and triumphs of young workers and students which is not necessarily conveyed to other members of staff unless there is a good record system. Leavers who achieve notable success academically are usually known in the staffroom, while young people who have obtained interesting jobs or qualified in their craft or profession frequently communicate their success to tutors. A good pastoral system should produce records of the destination of as many leavers as possible, sharing this information with the careers advisers. Tutors and careers teachers can between them provide the governing body or parents assembled on speech day with an analysis of the main courses and careers entered by the previous year's leavers. The extent to which this aim is achieved could be of the criteria by which a good school is assessed in its community.

Chapter 9
School–Industry Links

At one time vocational studies were frowned upon in many schools and teachers pretended not to know about the Saturday and holiday jobs done by their pupils. Any suggestion that education was designed to train people for work was as distasteful as the idea that the demands of industry and commerce might influence the curriculum and somehow betray the basic principles of education.

Many teachers undoubtedly had a very poor image of industry and still thought of the 'dark, Satanic mills' of nineteenth-century literature; some of them actively discouraged any pupils who expressed an intention to work in manufacturing industry. Commerce was not considered much better except that it was not so dirty or dangerous, but it conjured up a picture of young people pounding typewriters or undertaking boring clerical operations. When James Callaghan as Prime Minister made his Ruskin College speech in October, 1976, and the government Green Paper 'Education in Schools' advocated definite attempts to increase mutual understanding between education and the world of work, LEAs began asking headteachers if their schools had a policy on contacts with industry and commerce.

This was separate from the claims for better careers education and guidance, but allied to it; among other documents mentioning the need for more careers work was the British Institute of Management Working Party report, *Industry, Education and Management* (1979). This made a powerful plea for everyone working in industry and those guiding the attitudes of young people, to understand the background to industrial operations and the contribution which industry makes to the quality of life in our society. It was clearly felt that many teachers had no conception of the challenge of industrial careers for academically able youngsters. They were unaware of the intellectual satisfaction in solving problems, human and technological, the creativity needed to invent and market new products, the high responsibility involved in much financial

investment and management, together with sensitivity to the requirements of consumers while maintaining a sympathetic attitude to
employees' need for good working conditions and reasonable security.
The Green Paper expressly recognised the desirability of a school policy
'to help children to appreciate how the nation earns and maintains its
standard of living and properly to esteem the essential role of industry
and commerce in this process'. This was meant to apply across the
curriculum, separate from the demands of the working world for school-
leavers to achieve greater competence in mathematics, science and
technology.

Rapid growth of new materials and processes in industry and the
changing pattern of work resulted in large-scale redundancies which
included highly qualified workers. Increasing difficulty in obtaining any
work for young people leaving school forced schools to consider ways in
which the curriculum might be adapted to take account of the different
adult world for which pupils were being prepared. Emphasis upon
relationships between schools and community reinforced this trend as
local councillors and school governors expressed concern and so
influenced the attitudes of many teachers.

The word 'industry' in this context is not limited to manufacturing
establishments, but includes commerce, finance and the public services
if a whole-school policy on contacts with the world of work is to be
successfully implemented. Science, mathematics and CDT have direct
connections with many industrial processes, but all subjects can be
involved. Schools in rural areas, seaside towns or commercial centres
may feel that there is no need for them to be concerned with links with
industry because the surrounding community contains few manufacturing enterprises, but the term must be employed to cover all forms of
economic activity.

Secondary schools have for many years arranged for pupils to visit
local workplaces as part of their careers education and this has often
been extended into schemes of work experience to enable pupils to
perform some simple operation in order to acquire an idea of the
demands of employment. If real work is to be done it is naturally
confined to these simple operations requiring very little training or skill.
At first it was mainly offered to pupils of limited academic success.
Comparable schemes were sometimes offered during school holidays to
sixth-formers preparing for public examinations. Any opportunity for
pupils to gain insight into the working world should improve an
understanding of the economic structure of society, how employment is
generated, the role of export earnings to pay for imported goods and

industry's part in creating national wealth from which social services, including education, are paid for. Teachers taking parties of pupils to factories and offices have often returned to school with much useful material for classroom discussion on, for example, trade unions, organisational hierarchies, the disciplines of work, nationalised industries and private firms operated for profit, concepts of added value as raw materials become finished goods, the interdependence of workers with many different skills and functions, the excitement of risk taking, and so forth. If work experience does not enhance pupils' understanding, tolerance and consideration for others, it is largely failing in its main purpose.

National schemes

Headteachers can draw upon a number of national schemes for school–industry link activities besides the local contacts they have through the Careers Service, governors and the LEA. Among the best known are *CRAC Insight* programmes which enable sixth-formers to spend a week working on problems, simulations and business games in small groups led by a young manager from a local firm. Sixth-formers can follow two-day programmes under the *Industrial Society Challenge of Industry* or *Challenge of Enterprise* conferences. Here they work with young managers, listening to lectures, taking part in discussions and working through exercises to foster an understanding of industrial relations in a free society where managers must appreciate their relationships with workers and trade union branches.

The *Schools Curriculum Industry Partnership,* a national initiative locally operated, is intended to cover pupils of the whole ability range. It is dependent upon subject teachers influencing the curriculum by collaborative activities which include attachment to industry, exchange of personnel and ways of promoting experiential learning to prepare pupils for the teamwork demanded so commonly in industry.

Project Trident offers a combination of three one-week blocks of time comprising work experience, community service and some form of leisure activity. As with other extra-mural activities headteachers have sometimes been reluctant to release able examination candidates, but those who have found the scheme successful have claimed that work experience is not so educative on its own as when combined with the three-pronged Trident method.

Index offers six months' paid work in industry to academic highflyers who have obtained a place on a degree course and can use the gap between school and university not just to earn money but to have surpervised experience to develop their potential for later employment in a professional or managerial capacity. *GAP* arranges work placements overseas to cover this transition period.

The *Grubb Institute Transition to Working Life* project is particularly valuable in helping less academically successful pupils by arranging for working coaches drawn from the shop floor, rather than management, to take a small group of fifteen or sixteen year olds on a regular weekly basis to help them make the transition from school to work or a training programme under YTS.

Understanding British Industry is an offshoot of the CBI Educational Foundation and operates in selected areas as a liaison organisation arranging secondments of teachers to industry, their attendance at companies' management courses and the provision of classroom material.

Understanding Industry enables managers from industry and commerce to work on projects with pupils, sometimes during the period after the summer examinations, to provide insight into business operations and problem-solving techniques.

Young Enterprise provides all the necessary advice and documentation to enable a group of pupils to set up a mini-enterprise whereby they manufacture and market a product, financing the operation by selling shares to teachers, parents and friends of the school. In this way pupils simulate on a small scale the whole operation of a company, exercising leadership and consultation to acquire understanding of the inter-relationship of functions in an enterprise. Some schools have started their own mini-enterprises, often on the lines of a worker cooperative, as an alternative to using Young Enterprise. Others have taken initiative locally in other ways.

Curriculum Initiatives take many forms from single *twinning* arrange-ments with a local firm whereby representatives attend staff meetings to foster mutual understanding or provide materials and access to mainframe computers, for instance, to the weaving of a thread running through the whole curriculum and perhaps called Design or Science, Technology and Society. There are schemes specific to science depart-ments such as the help derived from a local SATRO (Science and Technology Regional Organisation), the School Technology Forum at Trent Polytechnic, the National Centre for School Technology, the Schools Information Centre on the Chemical Industry and others. Teachers of science and CDT are familiar with the resources provided by the SCSST (Standing Conference on Schools' Science and Technology) and from the education liaison managers of some of the best-known science-based companies. Many of these initiatives are financially assisted by industry and stem from its concern that young people should be better prepared at school for the realities of working life, even though many youngsters face a bleak outlook in areas of high unemployment. Both the CBI and TUC work to foster links with schools in order to improve industry's image and help pupils with later adjustment to work. On the educational side, the Schools Council and its successor, the Schools Curriculum Development Committee, have promoted initiatives to the same end. Examples are the Careers Education and Guidance Project, Skills for Working Life, the Industry Project and elements in the materials published as 'Geography for the Young School-leaver', 'Geography 14–18 project', Language in Use project' and 'English for Immigrant Children'.

Local initiatives

Headteachers keen to foster links with local firms will find it helpful first to obtain the cooperation of governors, parents, LEA members and senior staff of the Careers Service, as well as ensuring support from within the staffroom. Some have found it useful to set up a local committee or working party so that influential people can be involved from the start. Chambers of commerce, Rotary Clubs and other organisations can provide good contacts to supplement those of the careers officer. The local authority planning department may be able to spare some staff time to collaborate with teachers to produce interesting projects and materials. It may also employ an industrial development officer who will welcome the chance of helping teachers to promote the acceptability of school-leavers to new employers being attracted to the district.

Wherever employers can meet teachers informally there is certain to be some profitable outcome, if only in encouraging feedback to the staffroom of problems they may have encountered in training young workers. For too long employers have criticised schools for the apparently low standards of their leavers, but it is far more productive if a few training officers, foremen and supervisors can sit round a table with teachers and discusss the ways in which young people have not been able to cope with their training or have fallen down on the job. This has often led to interesting curricular developments and helped people in industry to appreciate the way school curricula and examinations are changing.

Teachers' extra-mural activities

While many teachers visit workplaces and arrange extra-mural experiences for their pupils, few *exchanges* take place between teachers and industrialists, who seldom accept invitations to visit schools. Where teachers are attached to industry for periods of several weeks, considerable organisation is needed to provide resources to cover their classes. As an example, Buckinghamshire LEA provided two supply teachers to stand in for teachers of science or technology accepting invitations to spend worthwhile periods acquiring ideas to adjust their curricula and sample materials. The CBI has a scheme for three-week secondments as an Introduction to Industry for teachers and some local school-industry liaison officers or industry–school coordinators arrange similar schemes from local sources. These will do no more than widen the horizons of individual teachers and perhaps enrich their classroom teaching, unless the headteacher deliberately arranges for those teachers to feed back to other members of staff the results of their industrial placements. A talk given at a staff meeting may attract some colleagues to apply for secondment and should contribute to reducing ignorance and prejudice.

A Hertfordshire CDT teacher exchanged jobs for a term with a training officer from a local high technology firm to the manifest benefit of both, and with the enthusiastic support of the headteacher and LEA. This type of exchange is not easy to carry out, but may increase if rolls continue to fall, enabling teachers of science, mathematics or business studies, for example, to benefit from this professional refreshment. British Petroleum pioneered the attachment of teachers for a whole term where they worked on problems such as entrance tests, recruitment standards or scientific and engineering problems.

In other cases senior teachers, including some headteachers, have been accommodated on companies' management courses where they have worked on projects with people of equivalent seniority and qualification so that they returned to school with new insights into their own managerial functions. Schools have been isolated for too long and many headteachers have talked sceptically about any possible comparability between their role and that of profit-oriented managers. In fact, most organisations function through people, whether their purpose is primarily to sell products or to exemplify the 'caringness' of which schools are so proud.

Teachers are not so innocent of the working world as some parents evidently imagine. Headteachers may not be aware of the past or present commercial experiences of their staff, yet most teachers have experienced work at low levels of skill during their sixth-form or college vacations even if they are not currently writing textbooks, running a business or working in the leisure industry during the holidays. An astonishing variety of working experiences is sometimes revealed at an interview for the position of head of careers, for instance, when it can be of real significance to the candidate's approach to the job. The careers department can make use of colleagues' previous experience, however short-term, to enrich the careers curriculum. While recognising that some teachers are so prejudiced against industry as a result of their youthful experiences, headteachers can encourage others to contribute to work in other departments, not only in careers, if they discover that there is a wealth of untapped resource within the staff.

Industrialists in schools

The traffic between school and industry may be mostly one-way, but there are ways in which teachers can use their own expertise to help outsiders. Instruction to managers on the techniques of public speaking, for example, would come very easily to a teacher who has been trained as a communicator, unlike most scientists, engineers or accountants. Teachers may need to help those representatives of the working world who are invited to come into school to talk to pupils about aspects of employment or personal financial planning because an audience of restless teenagers is very different from one of interested adults, even for a proficient public speaker. A few tips on how to keep boys and girls attentive and interested may double the impact of a stranger coming into the classroom, even though simple discipline will be covered by the presence of a teacher throughout the session.

Industrialists visiting schools are sometimes accused by unsympathetic teachers of trying to further their own recruitment of leavers or enlarging their list of customers, but there are often sound reasons for a personnel manager to want to look at the work done by pupils to gauge what can be expected of different age groups and ability levels in relation to the firm's training policy. Businessmen can happily be invited into school for informal lunches with staff and pupils, particularly if this follows a work experience scheme, and they can talk to teachers about the pupils' experiences and then sit in on classes or see pupils' work displayed about the school. It is equally valuable for shop stewards or trade union organisers to visit as 'associate teachers' to take classes through some aspects of industrial relations as part of a social studies or history course.

Outsiders can contribute interestingly to staff meetings when discussion is taking place on new training schemes for certain occupations or on school subjects and examinations in connection with industry and commerce. They may enjoy talking to house or year tutors about some of the social and personal problems which affect young people starting work. A forum of people from several firms can illuminate staff or parents' meetings by explaining the significance of news items about industrial relations or how conflict arises within the hierarchies of a workplace. Such topics need a firm chairperson, however, to prevent discussion degenerating into accusations about standards or ethos on either side.

Careers conventions

In addition to giving talks about working life, personnel managers have been welcomed in some schools to conduct mock interviews with pupils. On the other hand, many have only been invited into school in order to man a stand at an exhibition of local industry or for a careers convention. These conventions have now declined in popularity as a result of high unemployment and some organisations' unwillingness to take part. Some headteachers feel that these events do not repay the time and effort required to organise them.

Careers conventions have so often been biased towards careers requiring good examination passes or those mainly attractive to boys that a conscious effort has to be made to ensure that girls visit the stands featuring engineering and construction and boys realise that nursing is just as applicable to some of them. Careers conventions can be an excellent gloss on the careers education programme if pupils are properly prepared beforehand and there is significant follow-up afterwards. If a wide spread of occupations is represented they can really benefit by an afternoon or evening's attendance, especially if they have done some preliminary research into the entry requirements of occupations on which they propose to question the consultants.

Opinion among careers teachers differs on the methods of using careers conventions to best effect for pupils and parents. Should there be formal presentations from a platform, set times at which consultants give short talks in classrooms with the audience moving on when a bell rings, or a free-for-all with pupils and parents milling round until they find someone free to question about an occupation in which they are interested? If intensive follow-up classes lead to written work by the pupils and sharing in discussion of the knowledge they have acquired, the event can be justified as an educational activity whatever the outcome for any individual boy or girl. A badly run careers convention does real harm to the school's reputation as does apathy on the part of the youngsters or no provision being made for consultants' refreshment after their normal day's work. When it is well run, with pupils detailed to look after consultants and influential local people, much goodwill is generated in the community and later school–industry links will be facilitated. Headteachers should always be noticeably present themselves if the school is to reap the benefit of outsiders' goodwill in future.

Curricular significance

Employers' representatives need to be alerted on new curricular developments, especially if they are clearly seen as prevocational. BTEC courses are available in some schools in conjuction with colleges of further education, while many business studies courses include work experience in offices. City and Guilds, which employers associate with qualifications in skilled crafts, have infiltrated into secondary schools with foundation courses designed to capture the broad occupational interests of pupils before they have made a firm choice of a career. Both examining bodies have combined to provide CPVE assessments and new courses for boys and girls from the age of fourteen. At the same time the Royal Society of Arts, traditionally associated with high level office skills, has promoted vocational preparation courses for young people aspiring to clerical work. Amid all the choices, and consequent confusion, high hopes are pinned on the National Council for Vocational Qualifications whose efforts to rationalise the situation will have beneficial spin-off effects in the schools where young people are making their first tentative career choices.

Employers do not always appreciate that some times of year are much more practicable for school–industry link activities because of the cycle of examinations and other constraints. Boarding schools frequently leave these contacts to be carried out during vacations, especially when they involve periods of work experience or shadowing provided by parents, past pupils or other friends of the school who can offer programmes of 'windows on the nation at work'.

Teachers will find profiling, as a supplement or alternative to public examinations, less intimidating if they can consult some local employers on the qualities which they would like stressed and perhaps try out on them some sample profile systems to find what would be most acceptable. The City and Guilds profile system is a useful guide.

Some teachers have arranged discussions with local employers on the tests used for the selection of trainees. This is helpful to the careers department, but equally to teachers of mathematics, English or CDT, who may familiarise pupils with some of the concepts and techniques even though they will not be able to obtain actual current tests in use. The controversy over problems apparently caused when leavers schooled in metric mathematics find their employers still measuring in feet and inches or quarts and ounces can be turned to good account if employers can indicate in what limited mathematical calculations a knowledge of length or volume in imperial measure will be required so that pupils can be prepared. Simple instruction based upon the usage of certain local firms will forestall some of the complaints levied against the schools.

A whole-school policy on links with industry can be implemented in most subjects of the curriculum if a keen teacher is appointed to coordinate various extra-mural events. This may embrace responsibility for a twinning arrangement or an attempt to interest some teachers in each department in linking with industry, perhaps building on the known contacts made by teachers of CDT and business studies. The coordinator can get geography teachers attached to the local authority planning officers for a day or two, geologists to an oil company, linguists to travel agents and home economists to bakeries and hotels. Textile teachers can usefully observe clothing manufacturers and retailers, scientists connect with engineering firms and laboratories, mathematicians with accountants, banks, building societies and insurance offices, while biologists will have much scope within the health services. Teachers of English can study the language requirements in offices and assess the communication levels in different parts of industry, while historians may find time in a trade union office or company secretary's archive room as rewarding as research in a museum or county record office. PE teachers can promote the exchange of facilities with local businesses' recreational resources.

School–industry links will not be successful unless the headteacher is totally committed to their value and can persuade staffroom colleagues to make the necessary adjustments to enable individuals to respond to overtures from industry. Some LEAs have provided an extra part-time teacher to undertake the coordination. This has been especially helpful when opportunities are being sought for mildly handicapped pupils, each of whom may need personal approaches to employers for work experience or similar activities, or to expand the horizons of girls and reassure pupils from ethnic minorities that they can have the same opportunities for curricular enrichment as anyone else. The task of coordination may be entrusted by the headteacher to a senior colleague or the head of careers who may be considered suitably neutral, whereas teachers of economics, business studies, CDT or science may be thought to favour certain sectors of the economy. The coordinating teacher needs to be well versed in the administrative procedures required when pupils have experiential learning away from school premises. Close contact with the careers officer will be fruitful at all stages, together with any lecturers from local colleges who are already in touch with some teachers.

LEA industry school liaison officers (SILOs) or coordinators (DISCOs) have produced directories of extra-mural resources for schools in their area, slide-tape presentations and materials on local industries, besides guidelines on work experience and industrial visits. Teachers appointed to these posts enjoy considerable freedom of operation and have been notably effective in influencing relationships between schools and their community.

Headteachers asked to evaluate their school–industry links will not always find this easy apart from simply summarising activities undertaken by teachers and pupils. This experiential learning is seldom subject to formal examination unless the school enters candidates for 'Understanding Industrial Society' or certain economics papers. The headteachers may devise a means of assessing whether pupils have greater knowledge of work, the roles of industry in society, technological implications of jobs and perhaps a clearer appreciation of their own aspirations. Reports from heads of department may reveal the extent to which industry links have contributed to the formal and hidden curriculum and indicate whether pupils have progressed to better communication, reasoning and problem solving, analysis and objective observation, independent study, teamwork, dexterity and appreciation of human relationships among other possible attributes of a good programme.

Whether teachers' attitudes towards industry have changed depends upon many intangibles, including assumptions that industry links may have helped pupils to achieve acceptance of their own capacities, ambitions and attitudes towards authority and discipline. They may also have increased sensitivity to the needs of others and a willingness to cooperate in a team project, better understanding of the impact of work upon the lives of people encountered as strangers outside school and other aspects of employability and readiness to leave school. In the past contacts with the community have for many teachers been limited to parents, governors, staff and members of the LEA rather than the industral neighbours of the school. In rural settings schools have a harder task, but can substitute simulations, business games and other published materials to add to classroom learning from literature, drama, television and film to give opportunities to pupils to acquire insight into the human qualities of adult working life.

Work experience, observation, shadowing and sampling

It may be useful to distinguish the various types of industry-linked activities often lumped together under the term 'work experience' because some may be more appropriate in certain circumstances than others.

Work sampling enables pupils to try their hand at a job which they may later wish to enter as a permanent career. Individual boys and girls are encouraged to select two or three jobs after the normal process of self-assessment and careers information and guidance. Teachers then try to find appropriate opportunities for them as part of the total work experience programme of the fifth or sixth-year pupils. The experience should be valuable, whether the leavers take up the sampled career or not.

Work observation, sometimes called *trailing* or *shadowing*, enables pupils to attend a workplace in order to follow a worker or workers doing their various daily tasks, but not actually performing the operations themselves. Sixth-form pupils have often spent days in nursery or primary schools towards the end of their schooldays in order to decide whether they really wanted to train as teachers. Work observation is more satisfactory than mere visiting for an afternoon and is ideal for those hoping to train for a highly skilled craft or profession which they obviously cannot actually undertake themselves. It can include observing a voluntary worker's day or a creative artist working alone as well as employees of a company or public service. Shadowing enables teenagers to observe the work, decisions and responsibilities of top managers and directors.

Work experience is normally restricted to jobs at low levels of skill and training, but enables pupils during their last year of compulsory schooling to test themselves against the disciplines of a workplace, follow instructions and get on with adults outside their normal circle of friends and relatives. They have to find their way about a firm's premises, observe time-keeping rules, understand terminology and cope with tasks which may be initially frightening but, when conquered, confer a new sense of adulthood and confidence.

Work experience was recommended in the Newsom Report *Half Our Future* in 1963 and has become widespread since. Some schools have been able to give all fifth-form pupils a week of work experience; others limit it to those not making demonstrably good progress academically but whose teachers hope that its insight into the demands of industry might motivate to greater effort and attainment. It is becoming harder to get extensive work experience opportunities for school pupils owing to the demands on employers of the Youth Training Scheme. Headteachers are easily convinced of its value, however, as there is ample proof of its effect upon the standards of work and behaviour of many youngsters.

The original guidelines issued by the Department of Education and Science in Circular 7/74 may be worth quoting for staffroom discussion in any school contemplating starting a scheme:

> The principle which should underly any work-experience scheme is that pupils should be given an insight into the world of work, its disciplines and relationships. This principle and the requirements of the Act that schemes for pupils of compulsory school age must form part of an educational programme would not be satisfied by arrangements made, whether in school or elsewhere, whose purpose was specifically or mainly to assess individuals for particular forms of employment, or to occupy pupils in producing articles for sale. Schemes should include provision within the school curriculum for preparation before pupils take part in work experience and for following up and discussing the experience gained. Employers should be made fully aware of the aims of the scheme and should be invited to plan their part in cooperation with the schools.
>
> Work-experience should have value for pupils of varying ability and aptitudes and should neither be designed as vocational training nor aimed at a limited range of pupils only. If it is possible to arrange for a variety of types of work to be available, the opportunity for drawing comparisons will obviously be increased.

It would however be undesirable if the time spent by an individual pupil in any place of work was so short as to give a superficial impression. The total amount of time spent out of school on work experience schemes and its distribution will necessarily vary according to local and individual circumstances. In deciding how much time is appropriate, schools and local education authorities will need to take account of the time needed for supporting studies in school and to satisfy themselves that the total amount of time spent is appropriate within the educational programme of the pupils.

Many LEAs have issued guidelines and administrative memoranda to assist teachers starting work experience schemes. Headteachers having discussed with staff some of the issues involved, will need to nominate teachers to be responsible for the arrangements and monitoring of the scheme after checking its feasibility with officers of the Careers Service who have the necessary contacts with employers to suggest likely enterprises to approach. In areas where it has proved impossible to get realistic opportunities for more than a few pupils it may be possible to provide substitute experiences through local colleges of further education, especially if there are already good contacts with them. In this way pupils may be able to experiment with various tasks and use different materials, tools and processes. As a last resort, schools can use published simulation exercises.

Some teachers may object to the diversion of time, energy and resources into a work experience scheme on the grounds that many pupils in their last year of school already have considerable experience of the disciplines of work through their part-time and holiday jobs. The difference is, of course, that a work experience scheme undertaken in school time is essentially part of the pupils' total educational experience, whereas jobs are taken to earn money. Nonetheless, there is some definite maturing and learning process involved even in a newspaper round or Saturday selling job.

Other teachers may be unenthusiastic about work experience because they resent the absence of certain members of their classes or the departure of a whole year group at particular times. The purpose of the scheme must be clearly established if the headteacher is to get the support of all staff and their appreciation that this is an integral part of pupils' education, not part of the employers' selection process, and that pupils are not paid or trying to gain an advantage in the labour market over contemporaries who may not be included because they are sitting examinations. Work experience must not be considered a substitute for a proper programme of careers education and guidance; it is merely part of it and is clearly educational rather than vocational if a whole class or year group is included.

Headteachers may not always appreciate the amount of time needed to establish and control a work experience scheme. Several teachers will be involved if each pupil is to be visited while on employers' premises. There will also be a call for resources of stationery, fares, clerical help and hospitality for representatives of the organisations hosting the pupils.

Decisions have to be taken on the range of pupils included, methods of obtaining parents' approval, timing within the school year, and whether pupils are out for one day a week for a term or year or spend a complete week out each term. Staff must realise that it is not a way of getting rid of difficult or disruptive pupils or a carrot to prompt good behaviour by the threat of exclusion as punishment for misdemeanours! Staff will also discuss the relative merits of a free pupil choice of work to be observed or experienced, or direction by teachers deciding which opportunities will be most beneficial for particular boys and girls. Care must be exercised to watch for possible race and sex stereotyping if pupils are left to make their own free choices. It is especially valuable for pupils to go to several organisations to widen their occupational horizons. A well-constructed scheme, properly integrated into the educational programme, is of clear benefit to individual pupils and contributes to good relationships between the school and local community.

There are several published accounts of successful schemes of work experience. Readers are referred particularly to *Work Experience and Schools,* edited by A. G. Watts (Heinemann, 1983). See the Appendix to this book for addresses of national organisations promoting school–industry links.

Chapter 10

Examinations and Careers

It has become fashionable in some staffrooms for teachers to deplore their school's emphasis upon examinations which they attribute to parental pressure and the demands of employers and colleges of further education. Horror tales are told of boys and girls wracked with anxiety, unable to sleep, goaded by parents, jealous of successful siblings and generally reduced to scholastic incompetence by the strain of public examinations! Some teachers even maintain that the existence of examinations which some pupils may fail is contrary to the comprehensive ethos and a desirably more egalitarian society. Undeniably, examinations play a large part in the life of a secondary school and affect the school's policy on careers education and guidance. Even with the rationalisation inherent in the GCSE and initiatives to greater collaboration among vocational examining bodies, teachers responsible for guiding pupils and parents on appropriate goals have a hard task, while the staff tackling the administration, record keeping and monitoring of the process might well be daunted by the sheer size of the operation and complexity of examinations on offer.

When the teacher responsible for examination entries is also a member of the careers team, pupils may have more help in appreciating the connection between subject passes and the requirements of occupations. Too many still choose subjects at thirteen which two or four years later prove inappropriate for their developing career aspirations. All teachers should be reminded that it is the *lack* of a subject which may prove a barrier rather than the supposed *demand* for particular subjects. Exceptions are English and mathematics which are assumed to be needed for entry to most professions and courses of higher education. Lack of a pass in physics or chemistry or a language other than English is the commonest stumbling block, especially in the case of a late developer who may not have been considered very academic at thirteen, but blossoms in the run up to GCSE.

It should be pointed out to the antagonists of examinations that disadvantaged people have benefited by public examinations which eliminate patronage and nepotism, ensure fair treatment of candidates from different schools and counteract possible bias in an interview for a job or place on a course. Pupils from ethnic minorities can reasonably claim discrimination when they leave school if they have obtained good paper qualifications and still fail to get jobs in competition with less qualified indigenous contemporaries. The need for a school policy on examinations to be evolved after staff discussion has to be considered in the light of the academic inflation by which occupations have been raising their entry standards in what is becoming an increasingly credentialled society. Only the least academically able pupils and those who may be underachieving are immune from examination pressure, but the job market for them is shrinking with the disappearance of low-level manual work.

School examinations are big business. There were five and a half million subject entries when the situation was scrutinised by the Waddell Committee in 1977 and the number of subjects on offer exceeded two hundred. Many similar subjects have differing names, depending on the idiosyncrasies of the various boards. Before GCSE was instituted there were 230 subjects available for GCE and 120 for CSE. In practice, most boards examined in about thirty main subjects while some esoteric languages or variants on traditional subjects might only be available from one or two boards. Most schools consider between twenty and thirty subjects, having decided what they can offer from their resources of staff and equipment. Teachers understandably welcome the rationalisation of syllabi following the merger of GCE and CSE, however much some may regret the passing of a familiar system.

Parents who complain that their children are not being entered for the examinations which they believe lead to desirable forms of higher education or career sometimes forget that a youngster who leaves school with a string of examination passes may have worked hard, but may just have been fortunate to benefit from extremely good teaching. Moreover, examinations only assess the capacity to pass examinations and may bear no relationship to the demands of a job, though they are accepted as evidence of a pupil's ability to absorb knowledge, information and ideas with the capacity to withstand the strain of performing written or practical tests under strict time limitations.

New methods of examining

Teachers have been bombarded in recent years with arguments about criterion referencing or norm referencing. Much time has been spent considering ways to establish the criteria for acceptable competence at appropriate levels in different areas of the curriculum. Music is constantly quoted as a subject where pupils pass a succession of graded tests related to known standards of achievement and unconnected to the time spent on acquiring that standard or competition from other candidates. Researchers and officials of examining boards publish studies to reassure the public that every effort is made to establish fair systems of assessing competence in different subjects and between different examinations in the same subject. It is doubtful whether any system can measure exactly the amount of effort required to obtain a certain grade in, for example, art, chemistry and French, but at least those responsible are aware of the difficulties and do their best to allay public scepticism.

Despite the move towards more continuous assessment in place of a week of traumatic formal examinations at the end of a course, it is still not clear whether the new methods are more successful in picking out those young people who most deserve selection for a course or training in employment. Some college students who chose courses where they would be subject to continuous assessment in place of traditional examinations have regretted their decision when they felt under too much tutorial supervision throughout their course.

An additional reason for advocating new methods of examining was the expectation that multiple-choice questions or project assignments might overcome the cultural bias inherent in three-hour essay papers when taken by candidates from ethnic minorities or non-English speaking homes. Special consideration is sometimes claimed for pupils who suffer from hay fever or dyslexia in addition to arrangements for those who are medically assessed as in some way handicapped for examination purposes. All these points are likely to come up at a staff meeting on examination policy. In the end, two-thirds or more of the pupils in any secondary school are going to sit public examinations in the summer term of their fifth year and probably for the next two years if they remain in education. One of the most cogent arguments for raising the school-leaving age rehearsed in the Crowther Report *15 to 18* in 1960 was the identified wastage of young people with the potential to obtain qualifications and higher education because they were then permitted to leave school a year before sitting for a public examination. There are still, unfortunately, some able youngsters who leave at Easter because the law permits and they do not feel it worth while to stay at school another term in order to take a few subjects when they will then be competing for jobs and training opportunities with contemporaries who have been more successful.

Examinations for employment

It is reasonable to suppose that universities, polytechnics and other colleges and institutes of higher education have sufficient knowledge of school examinations to make their entry requirements realistic. This cannot always be said of employers who misuse school examinations as a way of simplifying their selection procedures. A certain number of passes in set subjects may legitimately be demanded of those recruited to careers in which they will be expected to sit for the examinations of professional bodies or take courses in a further education college leading to clerical, craft or technician qualifications. But in conditions of high unemployment many employers demand passes at levels that bear no relationship to the requirements of the job simply because they may be getting several hundred applications for each vacancy.

Tales abound in school staffrooms of employers' ignorance of the various grades and modes. There is bias towards traditional examinations and over-emphasis on long-standing academic subjects in preference to those newer areas of the curriculum which may be more vocationally relevant, but were not taken when selectors were themselves at school. Headteachers and their staff may dislike examinations for distorting the curriculum and creating problems for pupils and teachers, but recognise that they will continue to be used to assess potential for training and further education.

Careers teachers should take every opportunity to explain to staffroom colleagues the entry standards of the occupations commonly entered by leavers from that school. Parents need this information, too; it should be of concern to governors also. Heads of all subject departments should have syllabi of courses in higher and further education which have some connection with their subject, whether they are preparing pupils for examinations or not. Teachers of mathematics or history, for example, usually have a good knowledge of the entry requirements and course content for degrees in their own subject discipline. It is just as important for teachers to understand what City and Guilds or Royal Society of Arts examinations involve or where a B/TEC course may be beyond the capability of a youngster who is not doing particularly well in English and mathematics.

The school careers department should have examples of the syllabi of all the main examinations which young people leaving the school may be expected to take in later years. This information should be distributed widely among appropriate colleagues. Some of the issues for discussion before a school's policy on examinations is formulated concern facts on what occupations require what pass levels in which subjects (because these affect timetabling and resourcing). The extent to which the policy may unfairly handicap some leavers when they apply for a course or job should also be considered, however.

Careers teachers may also arrange for help to be given to pupils struggling for lack of appropriate study skills. Published materials relevant to this problem are available and may be tackled under general studies or in tutorial periods. Tutors may be encouraged to give formal preparation for examinations to alleviate the natural nervousness which inhibits many good candidates from performing well; this may be due to parental or peer group pressure, external circumstances, sickness, injury or domestic crisis. Much effort is expended by careers teachers to help young people to face interviews but, in a laudable attempt to reduce the trauma of examinations, teachers may give the impression that these are not important. Some youngsters who have done badly claim afterwards that they were not told they could have done well had they tackled the questions more sensibly and received advice on methods of revision and ways to relax their muscles in order to write for three hours.

Profiling

Every year more young people leave school with a formal profile of their achievements. Employers are getting used to this form of assessment, but many remain doubtful of the relevance to their recruitment of some of the profiles presented by applicants for jobs and training places. It is incumbent upon careers teachers to help their colleagues to produce meaningful records of pupils' competencies and ability so that they have some positive document to hand to a prospective employer or college admissions officer. Some LEAs have produced standard profile forms after consultation with teachers, careers officers and employers. City and Guilds has a well-researched form of profiling which can be used in schools as well as for trainees in work and further education. If an individual school is producing its own profile form it is desirable for a working party to be set up to discuss its detailed design. The head of careers would be an appropriate person to chair this group and should try it out on a few local employers at the pilot stage before it is printed in quantity. Experience with CPVE is obviously relevant.

As a guide to possible headings for discussion with tutors the following are suggested items which would interest employers: physical attributes, strength, vision, clear speech, manual and finger dexterity; neat handwriting; ability to talk, listen, read and write competently; sufficient numeracy to add, subtract, multiply and divide as well as measure accurately; understanding of written and spoken instructions; potential for training; ability to work without supervision and under time constraints; teamwork; initiative, energy and willingness to tackle new tasks; responsibility for tools, money, safety, materials; punctuality and time-keeping; politeness, courtesy and consideration for others; pride in good workmanship; and evidence of practice in problem solving.

Selection tests

With increasing competition for jobs, more employers may set their own tests for suitability for training. Firms in the computer industry do so, for example, and so do some large retailers and engineering companies selecting craft and technician trainees. Careers teachers can sometimes find out more by following up leavers after they have started work in order to prepare present pupils better. Teachers sometimes complain about inappropriate tests used by some recruiters and it is helpful if careers staff can discuss with recruitment and training personnel in industry and commerce the type of tests likely to be imposed upon their pupils when applying for training. For obvious reasons employers and test agencies do not readily give teachers examples of tests they are currently using, but one can sometimes get hold of comparable tests used in previous years just as one can obtain past examination papers. Wherever possible careers teachers should warn pupils that they may be confronted by a formal test when they go for a job interview.

Vocational relevance of examinations

TVEI schemes exemplify the modern emphasis upon vocational relevance in the school curriculum which is further illustrated by the introduction into secondary schools of examinations previously associated with further education. This poses a new responsibility upon careers teachers and pastoral staff involved in guidance. If pupils are choosing to take a course leading to B/TEC, City and Guilds or RSA examinations, they need insight into the nature of the course and examination, together with possible limitations which the timetable may impose upon their ability to take those school examinations which traditionally prepare for certain degree and diploma courses. The converse may also apply. Pupils on TVEI schemes need watching in case they are limiting their chances by particular examination goals.

Headteachers expect their careers staff to be closely involved at each decision point facing pupils from the age of thirteen. Some subjects are more useful than others. All possible applicants for degree courses should be persuaded of the need for passes in GCSE in English and mathematics. The vocational utility of physical sciences is obvious. A broad and balanced education is clearly desirable for all and should include study of aesthetic and creative subjects with practical, three-dimensional work and problem solving. Some pupils will not need to take all their subjects in public examinations and a progressive school may have a policy that examinations are taken by those pupils who need them for the next stage in their education or want to achieve evidence of successful application but not simply to 'tot up passes', to the detriment of their general educational and personal development.

Chapter 11
Preparation for Life After School

In answer to the question 'What happened to last year's leavers?' many teachers are embarrassed to be unable to provide more than a sketchy, anecdotal answer. It is easy to set up a record system, but not so easy to get the cooperation of the young people themselves, some of whom are so delighted to have left school that they have no intention of filling in a questionnaire or even returning to receive a prize or certificate.

Are they ready to leave school?

A useful topic for staffroom discussion is a set of criteria by which to assess pupils' readiness to leave school. One of the sad features of British secondary schools is the determination of so many youngsters to leave as soon as the law allows, even though their parents and teachers believe they are not ready for the adult world. Subject teachers may say that some boys and girls are unable to communicate or calculate and should not be permitted to leave school until they have achieved that measure of basic competence. Another benchmark might be self-reliance or personal autonomy; freedom from dependence upon parents, older siblings or friends. Can they cope with the necessary life and social skills expected of adults? Do they understand the ramifications of hire purchase, taxation, insurance and social security entitlement?

One important criterion is employability. Sadly, one can see some pupils in many fifth-form classes who are not really employable even if there were jobs available. Employability is a concept which may vary according to the labour market in different places, but those youngsters who appear to have failed to master elementary literacy and numeracy, have few social skills and an unfavourable attitude towards work may also be dubbed unemployable in present circumstances.

Young people are not ready to leave school if they have not thought about further study, attending a youth centre to develop a hobby or interest or appreciate the need for continued education in connection with a job they might get. They should have knowledge of the community's colleges and institutes and be prepared to consider trying them. They should have used the facilities of school to develop hobbies, sports or other activities so that they can make good use of increased leisure. A school whose leavers have not acquired any skills or developed interests and talents may be said to have failed many of its pupils.

Helping youngsters to acquire social and life skills with which to cope with adult life is not the sole province of the careers department, but its teachers will have a major part to play in the total scenario. These hapless youngsters must be assissted to overcome their sense of failure academically by success in other directions.

A leaver's kit

All boys and girls reaching the end of their fifth-year course should have covered work in their careers education programme so that they take away with them a survival kit for the next stage. This applies whether they remain in the sixth form, transfer to a college or try their luck in the job search or on a youth training scheme. Many schools issue a folder into which the pamphlets given out by various official sources can be stored, together with worksheets created by the careers teachers or produced to accompany video recordings and textbooks. The aim should be to provide leavers with all the information they might need when confronted by unemployment, job applications or leaving home at some future stage when they are out of touch with school. The Careers Service and local education authority publish information on various local services and it is not difficult to build up a complete set of leaflets on courses, social security and benefits, guides to income tax and insurance. All of this can be clipped together and put safely away in the folder which may be more carefully kept if it is of good quality and emblazoned with the school badge or motto. Lists of opening times of important local offices, the job centre and careers office, with a map of the area and public transport details, should be included.

Pupils should equip their folders with model curriculum vitae and letters of application for jobs. If they have practised this exercise they will be confident of doing it on their own later on. Names and addresses of suitable (and willing!) people who can be quoted as referees in future should be added, together with some notes on interview practice and possible questions to ask the interviewer if invited to do so. Some careers teachers use classes to make glossaries of useful terms, such as technician, shop steward or personnel manager and run through the most likely examinations young workers and students may encounter. The folder should also contain the results of any vocational aptitude tests, interest inventories or computerised guidance exercises the pupils have undergone during the course. Information on opening times of the public library can be added to booklists of reference works and titles of local and national newspapers and trade journals which may be consulted there. The kit should provide space for updating the information from time to time, noting works numbers which may be required during periods of sickness absence and the individual's national insurance and medical number. In addition it can contain examples of calculations done in class to work out the difference between what a job is stated to be worth and the weekly or monthly sum actually received after deductions.

Preparing for a harder world

The school's policy on homework, punctuality and attendance may need to be toughened during pupils' last year to prepare them for a hard and unsympathetic world outside. Teachers naturally encourage their charges wherever possible, but false praise for low standards of work and behaviour may not be in their best interests if it means slack standards when leavers start work or training. Teachers tell pupils when they have done better one week than the last, but to praise a youngster who has managed to get four out of ten exercises correct is poor preparation for work in industry and commerce when ten out of ten will be required of anyone checking the day's takings or sorting out supplies from a warehouse. It is incumbent upon the careers teachers to use their contacts to invite representatives of the working world to meet staffroom colleagues and explain to them the reasons why so many youngsters are often unhappy when they start work or training or leave jobs which they could cope with because they had not been expected to work at school to standards approximating to those of industry. Tutors and subject teachers can encourage their colleagues to stretch pupils as far as possible and insist on the best work of which they are capable. If this is neglected parents have a reasonable complaint that their children were not properly prepared for the demands of the working world.

Special courses of preparation for adult life

Headteachers concerned about those leavers with minimal qualifications who are going to have most difficulty in coping with adult life and possible long periods of unemployment may question the wisdom of subjecting these boys and girls to the normal academic programme of traditional school subjects. Some schools are, therefore, offering courses specifically designed to foster life and social skills on the lines first proposed by the Further Education Unit in *A Basis for Choice*. Many teachers are capable and keen to teach modules which may bear no relationship to their qualifications and main teaching subject, but derive from hobbies or interests. Periods of residential experience and community involvement can enliven an otherwise arid programme for unwilling scholars, while a scheme for pupils to tackle modules of learning on a block basis, for perhaps two afternoons a week can be attractive and productive. Pupils study the modules until they and their teachers agree that they are ready to be assessed as competent by someone from local industry, hospital or a voluntary agency, for example. If a certificate can be issued or the modules form part of a leaver's profile, this will give added confidence to pupils who will not have the automatic sense of achievement from examination passes, but may thereby be helped to meet the demands of adult life in the home, workplace and community.

Training in simple domestic tasks may be considered the proper responsibility of parents who are often influential in encouraging their children to acquire hobbies and interests. Many useful competencies can be developed within the school curriculum, however, given sufficient flexibility in timetabling and staff deployment. While perhaps of most significance for low-achievers, these learning modules should not be confined to them. Clever boys and girls can acquire the appropriate level of competence in less time than their slower schoolfellows and so acquire the certificates (which one hopes the school will have designed) to exemplify a comprehensive ethos which takes account of the varying speed at which adolescents learn.

Competencies for adult life may be primarily practical, mental or social and many are inherent in the programmes of the Boy Scouts, Girl Guides and Duke of Edinburgh's Award Scheme. Youngsters who excel at games may represent their school or club, while others publicly display their talents in art, music, drama and dancing. Competence in a range of life and social skills will enhance the employability of some leavers and make their schooling seem more relevant to the adult lives to which they look forward.

The development of competencies

Practical competencies which most pupils could profitably acquire include: basic cookery; household maintenance; first aid and home nursing; parent preparation and child development; car driving and maintenance; gardening; animal care; needlecraft; and personal type-writing, computer operating and office procedures. All pupils should have had an opportunity to design and make a functioning object so that they experience the translation of a design or pattern into a finished product. They should also have sampled a range of physical activities in addition to team games and gymnastics.

Mental competencies include keeping simple accounts; budgeting; principles of insurance; hire purchase; map-reading in town and country; the ability to understand graphic information–plans, blueprints, graphs, diagrams, working drawings from do-it-yourself manuals; environmental appreciation by observation and recording of natural phenomena, scenery, architecture, geology, flora and fauna, archaeol-ogical sites, meteorology; consumer protection; health and safety regulations; and citizenship, law enforcement, voting procedure and provision for emergencies.

Social competencies are acquired through many school activities and such subjects as English, drama, home economics and physical education. Four particular modules would increase self-confidence and enrich adult life: public speaking; committee procedure; communication in another language; community service.

The individual modules of learning designed to develop these competencies can be taught by teachers from any department who are keen to tackle them. Some others might be covered after school by outsiders as, for example, when car driving is taught by police officers or first aid by nurses. The head of careers may assume responsibility for coordinating offers from colleagues and invitations to outsiders, thus enlarging his or her role as the instigator, but not sole provider, of that part of the careers programme devoted to preparation for adult, but not necessarily working, life.

Helping pupils choose a career

Despite the high unemployment facing many young people it is legitimate to assume that most people will be able to work for part if not all of their adult life. Life and social skills are not a sufficient basis for choosing a career, so headteachers may like to be reminded of the main factors which experienced careers advisers take into account when helping pupils to make a career choice–one of the most important decisions any of them will have to make as teenagers or adults.

There are some *physical* factors which may affect people's ability to fit into the working world. Height and weight affect the chance of becoming a police officer or jockey, for instance. Poor eyesight (particularly colour vision) or hearing, physical handicap and sickness record may be indicative of jobs to avoid.

Educational attainments and potential have to be considered particularly by those ambitious to enter one of the professions where there are entry requirements and examinations to be taken before qualifying.

Some *skills* acquired during schooldays may be relevant to work or indicative of capability for training. Keyboarding, shorthand or technical drawing have obvious utility. Practical classes may have developed good manual or finger dexterity, and a youngster who has passed a test to ride a motorcycle may be able to get work more easily than another who has not. Skill in music, acting or painting may commend a leaver to employment if this is listed on a testimonial or profile.

Interests are usually paramount in the minds of boys and girls considering their future careers, and teachers are becoming more familiar with the psychologically based inventories which can be administered to teenagers to assess the real strength of their stated interests. Many people underline 'music' on a list of interests, for example, but do not play an instrument or sing in a choir, seldom attend concerts and spend little spare cash on records and cassettes. They give 'music' as an interest simply because they normally work against a background of Radio One. A class of pupils can be prompted to assess whether their individual interests betray them as social or solitary people, practical, bookish or energetic, and so on.

Family circumstances need to be treated with delicacy, but are frequently important either because there is a real need for another contributor to the family finances or because there may be job opportunities in a family business or profession. Strong family pressure to enter or avoid a particular occupation needs watching by sensitive tutors and careers advisers.

Personal qualities and *abilities* are usually best known to tutors and are obviously important in many careers. Independence of spirit, self-confidence and the desire to travel may be identified as indicating an adventurous character who may be drawn to certain ways of life. The most important quality for success in nearly all careers, however, is the ability to get on with people.

Ideals and *values* are strong motivators for some young people who may choose a career because it appeals to their desire to promote a political, religious or social cause. Each youngster has to work out a value system for deciding on one path rather than another. Is high pay more important than other aspects of a job and would one do a dull, dangerous or dirty job just because it paid well? Do future prospects compensate for low pay while under training? Is the security of a slow progression up a salary scale preferable to the higher rewards of a risky enterprise? Is the status of the occupation or employer important? There are many factors to be weighed up and a good programme of careers education should provide a framework for the decision-taking process.

Teachers who question the purpose of careers education can be challenged to consider their own value system and the extent to which teaching fulfils their aspirations and attributes. To some extent the ethos of the school determines whether the self-understanding part of preparation for adult life is the prime responsibility of form tutors, careers teachers or teachers of social education or religious education. Tutors have special relationships with their groups and can use tutorial time flexibly to cover some of these topics. On the other hand, a more formal scheme of work should ensure that every pupil has given attention to the factors which affect choice of a career and can look forward to taking decisions as wisely as possible. Some of them know what they want to do as adults. It may be to share in the prosperity of a working group or risk self-employment; to influence, control, persuade or manipulate others; to work in a small firm or large organisation; to travel or work abroad; to involve one's family, have congenial colleagues or a pleasant environment; to have varied tasks, acquire skills or advance knowledge; pit oneself against physically demanding work, help people or sell to them; to be a public servant or private entrepreneur. All these and many more can be identified as motivating factors which some young people recognise in themselves when they come to terms with choices to be made.

Topics for staff discussion

1. When should careers education start? In year one, two or three? How much time should it have in these years?
2. How can the options scheme be arranged so that it minimises constraints on pupils' choices of higher education and careers?
3. What mechanisms are most appropriate for coping with it?
4. What practical outcomes follow from a decision to devote a certain amount of time and resources to TVEI and other prevocational elements in the curriculum?
5. How can the school implement a policy of allocating 2.5 per cent of pupils' time in years three, four and five to careers education?
6. Which teachers will teach what elements in the programme?
7. The role of tutors in preparing pupils for adult and working life needs defining. How much are they to contribute to the careers programme? Do they keep records, write testimonials and references, undertake educational and career guidance?
8. What are the consequences for a full programme of careers work if the school is on more than one site?
9. If the head of careers produces a calendar of proposed careers events, what significance has this for staff colleagues?
10. What contribution can the head of careers make to staff INSET?
11. An inventory of the school's resources for careers, both physical and human, may be revealing. Are computers used effectively? What suggestions have newcomers to the staff?
12. Can the careers officer and lecturers from FE colleges make a significant impact upon staff meetings? How welcome would they be?
13. What should be contained in a leavers' survival kit?
14. Pupil records are a sensitive topic. Who could lead a discussion on confidentiality, custody, responsibility for monitoring, their use as a resource for references and application forms for higher education, ingredients for profiles?
15. Can past pupils make an effective contribution to present pupils' careers curriculum? If so, how? What is known among staff of their destinations, successes and failures?
16. What are the organisational consequences of various proposals for increasing school–industry links for teachers and pupils?
17. If a decision is taken that all fifth-year pupils shall have a week's work experience, how is this to be organised?

18. Reviewing the school's policy on examinations, are there any features which narrow pupils' choice of career? How can this be overcome? Have staff sufficient knowledge of the commoner vocational examinations taken by young workers and students after they have left school? Does this knowledge lead to any modification in curriculum? Are ten GCSE passes at low grades better than four good passes? Is fast-stream entry a year ahead of the age cohort justified? Are retakes encouraged? Is there a case for extra tuition after school for additional minority subjects or improved performance?

19. Is the school's policy on equal opportunities and racism awareness working successfully in preparing pupils for leaving?

20. What contributions can individual members of staff make to the development to social and life skills and acquisition of basic competencies? How can this be accomplished?

PART III
PROBLEMS AND SOLUTIONS

Chapter 12

Constraints

However much teachers believe in a whole-school policy for careers education and guidance, the circumstances of many schools impose constraints on its implementation, even when agreed by all the staff. There are difficulties in many areas simply because of the environment in which the school is situated. If it is a very poor area it will be hard to persuade able boys and girls to continue in full-time education to the age of eighteen and beyond. If there is a very high level of local unemployment, declining industries, many parents out of work and a generally depressed situation, it will be harder to persuade everyone that careers is a proper subject for the curriculum and that it contains much more than mere job information.

Falling rolls

Where there is a marked fall in pupil numbers one of the consequences will be difficulty in preserving the desirable breadth of curriculum. Headteachers will have problems in ensuring that all pupils receive adequate careers education. Their very proper concern to provide appropriate education in sciences, languages, humanities and creative arts for all young people at a time when the staffing ratio may be worsening, may make it harder to provide for non-examination subjects such as careers. Subjects relegated to part-time teachers, a consortium arrangement or links with a further education college may impose extra difficulties. Falling rolls have the additional consequence that head-teachers are not able to advertise a vacant post for head of careers, but have to make an internal appointment. The person appointed may have little real enthusiasm for the task and will need training, just when it is particularly difficult to release teachers to attend the courses offered by the LEA or an outside agency. The quality of the careers education and guidance may suffer in a laudible attempt to ensure at least some quantitative provision.

Smaller numbers in the main school and even smaller ones in the sixth form make it more likely that older pupils will have their careers classes on a mixed-ability basis, especially if the work is tackled in tutor groups. It is socially desirable for boys and girls covering the whole range of academic ability to discuss their futures together and I have consistently campaigned for the future manager or professional practitioner to work on projects with other young people who may be lucky to get any job at all. In reality this is difficult to achieve successfully unless the teachers are experienced, have ample resources for individual work and the school has a tradition of mixed-ability teaching. Otherwise the discussions can be hurtful to sensitive pupils as they discuss their differing future prospects. Teachers have a duty to encourage pupils who have the capacity to obtain qualifications and aspire to higher education, while avoiding a heightened sense of failure in those who are only likely to obtain a few modest GCSE passes. Yet the constraint is there as numbers decline.

Another limitation imposed by the socio-economic background of schools may inhibit the use of governors, local councillors and members of education committees from contributing to the schools' careers programmes and offsetting the effect of falling rolls. If parents and other friendly adults are themselves unemployed or only fitfully employed they are probably embarrassed to be asked to talk to classes and unable to offer opportunities for work experience or shadowing. It is increasingly difficult for small parties of pupils to visit workplaces or training establishments when there is a shortage of teachers to accompany them. Headteachers may request members of staff to cooperate by sharing their individual programmes of extra-mural activities, but this may not happen if there is little opportunity for staffroom discussion and inter-departmental arrangements.

The Careers Service

The resources provided by the LEA for the Careers Service may also be variable and in themselves constrain the schools' use of this critical agency. Traditionally, careers officers interviewed all pupils during their fourth or fifth year besides participating in the programme of classroom lessons. Many careers officers have latterly withdrawn from classroom group work and confined their school function to interviewing selected pupils at decision-taking points in their progress. This is understandable, given the pressures upon careers officers from their role in connection with the Youth Training Scheme, but it limits the range of expertise available to careers teachers searching for ways to make their subject interesting and varied.

In some places the careers office has been sited on a school premises, to obvious advantage for pupils, but possible discouragement of those who have left and wish to sever all connection with school. In most places one or more careers officers was in attendance at each secondary school on known days on a weekly or fortnightly basis, spending the rest of their time in the careers office. Now it is more usual for the system of 'bulk interviews' to be replaced by referral by the careers teachers of those pupils who apparently need more specialised help than is available within the school. In some areas all interviews with careers officers take place at the office. The 1987 annual careers conference was devoted to the theme of 'Working Together' (the title of the preparatory document commended by the three Secretaries of State for Education, Employment and Wales), but careers officers can only collaborate with their teacher colleagues if they themselves are resourced accordingly. Pressure on them to give more help to the unemployed and adults imposes another restraint upon their capacity to respond to invitations from schools.

Teachers' role

Careers education is essentially a form of experiential learning although it has its conventional cognitive elements. It is eminently suitable for small group work, but this may be quite impossible to organise if there is a shortage of available teachers. It is a teacher-intensive subject if there is a wide variety of activities involving external resources, yet teachers may have limited non-teaching time to organise this. Many teachers, moreover, feel unhappy about their counselling role if they have not had any specific training for it, but all tutors and careers teachers find themselves at times undertaking a counselling function. Some teachers' sense of inadequacy for the demands of careers work, and the limitations upon training opportunity, impose constraints upon the headteacher's ability to deploy the staff where need arises and enrich the programme of careers education.

Time

The biggest constraint is time. There is not enough time for the pupils to have access to a computerised job-information system such as JIIG-CAL and the chance to work through the many programs now available for use on micros. Time constraints prohibit many of the most interesting forms of school–industry link activities in less fortunate schools or those where public examinations loom disproportionately. Time for the teachers is even more constraining.

Careers teachers need more non-teaching time than many of their colleagues because they are expected to supervise and arrange external activities which may include work experience and shadowing, besides administering a department which affects almost all other departments in the school at some times and necessitates communication and record keeping of some sophistication if the programme is not to become chaotic. If the school believes in testing pupils in addition to normal examinations there may be an additional burden on the careers department. Careers will not be regarded seriously as a subject if the pupils do not do written work and have it properly corrected and marked.

Status

It is extremely difficult for a careers teacher to be effective if he or she has low status in the school hierarchy. With falling rolls and reduced prospects for teachers' promotion by moving to another school, headteachers can hardly expect a member of staff to take on responsibility for careers education without reward. Yet this is a comparatively new subject and the structure of the school may not have included this post, so that responsibility for careers is added to an existing responsibility in another subject or pastoral area. It can then get lost if that teacher leaves or is promoted within the school. If the head of careers has low status or is regarded as inexperienced or a has-been, it will be harder to obtain the cooperation of those members of staff on whom the programme depends if it is to be a truly integrating cross-curricular undertaking.

Examinations

A notable constraint is the pressure of examinations, especially when parents are known to be anxious for their children to achieve as many paper qualifications as possible. Examinations open doors to careers opportunities; one recognises parents' concern. But schools with a tradition of examination success sometimes relegate careers education to the less academically successful pupils, leaving the cleverer to make do with an interview for individual guidance. It should be obvious that detailed guidance will be required by those young people who will be competing for entry to universities and professions, but they also need the general discussions about work and self-marketing which are prescribed for classes of younger leavers. Indeed, the very complexity of subject and level requirements for entry to higher education means a greater need for factual information for these pupils than for many of those going into the YTS at sixteen or, if they are lucky, a local job.

Timetabled classroom careers education may be concentrated on those whose course is less examination orientated because they have the time. Many teachers may also feel that the problems of these pupils require sympathetic attention whereas the abler youngsters can postpone decisions because they are remaining in education longer. Occasionally this has disastrous consequences when they apply for higher education or professional training and find they have taken the wrong subjects for lack of guidance. Falling rolls impose further constraints on examination entries, particularly for 'A' level and Highers, while school policy on entering pupils for AS levels in minor subjects needs careful research to ensure that by so doing pupils are not disadvantaged in applying for particular degree courses later on. The proliferation of prevocational examinations may also be a constraint upon the grouping of suitable pupils for various careers activities.

If the teachers giving guidance to university candidates are not part of the careers team the subject may lose status in the eyes of parents and pupils and a divisive element may creep into the sixth form because those taking one-year CPVE and other courses are advised by the careers teachers. Headteachers need to survey who undertakes the tasks of record keeping, writing leavers' references and testimonials, profiles, the guidance to pupils on choosing TVEI programmes as well as prevocational courses to see what constraints these may impose on the effective working of the careers department. Some schools manage to overcome these problems, but all need to recognise the potential constraints they may impose on successful careers education and guidance.

Chapter 13

Issues

The careers department

There are many issues for discussion in a curriculum development committee looking into the school's policy for careers or to use as the core of an in-service training programme. What is the department to be called, for example? Is it sensible to talk about careers education when for so many young people non-work may be a more realistic future than paid work in the conventional sense? We need to redefine what we mean by 'careers' to ensure that other teachers do not misconstrue the work as mainly concerned with job information which was perhaps the case two decades ago.

Headteachers have to weigh the extent to which guidance, counselling and careers education overlap in order to avoid some pupils receiving excessive help while others may be denied what they need. Individual guidance is very time-consuming for teachers, but is clearly essential for many pupils at certain times. Careers education should be provided for all. The hidden curriculum and pastoral structure may emphasise the ethos of the school, but what effect does it have on pupils' attitudes towards work, wealth creation, society, the environment, politics and economics, for instance?

To what extent does the headteacher expect the careers department to undertake school–industry liaison activities and promote an infusion of industrial and commercial resources into the curriculum? It may be disastrous in the eyes of some colleagues if this development is associated with the career choices of the pupils rather than their education in technological literacy and basic economic understanding. Yet the head of careers often seems the most suitable person to take on these tasks. Work experience and shadowing is a particular case in point.

A delicate issue may arise from the headteacher's proposals for the way pupils are grouped for their careers education, by tutor groups based upon surnames, original entering groups by primary schools, ability or potential or even by expressed career interests or educational intentions.

Does the school's ethos as a caring institution doing its best for all pupils regardless of their strengths and weaknesses accord with the fact that adult society is often highly competitive? How should the careers department deploy its resources to provide individual pupils with access to guidance and counselling at times of need, with the overall requirement to establish a recognisable curriculum taking account of adolescents' normal progress towards vocational maturity?

Should the headteacher encourage colleagues who have acquired useful contacts to place favoured leavers in employment or should that task be firmly delegated to the careers officers with the consequence that these youngsters will then be in competition with leavers from other schools in the district?

A vital issue is the extent to which careers education is undertaken by tutors in pastoral time or taught in the timetable like geography or science. If it is timetabled, is it better to be covered in a weekly period or in blocks of half-days to give greater flexibility?

While it is obviously desirable to follow up leavers to find out what has happened to them, for how long is this practicable? It is useful to know the jobs or YTS placements they first entered or their choice of further and higher education, but this information may not give a true picture of their career intentions because so many change direction within the first year after leaving school or college. Even university careers services only publish statistics on first destinations of graduates, which may not reflect their ultimate career pattern.

If it is decided that the school should mount a careers convention or exhibition how can it be organised to avoid discouraging the less able pupils when experience indicates that employers are more interested in attracting the attention of those most likely to achieve academic successes. Conventions are costly to the consultants so one has to appreciate their view, but it is essential to recognise the problem and try to persuade those who will later offer training to the less successful leavers that they should attend.

How does a headteacher decide whether the programme of visiting speakers is to be open to particular groups or not? Is it preferable to present an unaccustomed speaker with a large audience of bored conscripts or a small number of enthusiasts?

If many departments want access to a limited number of micros or computer terminals, who decides the priorities and how does the careers department explain the considerable time required for each pupil to work through a range of programs on careers?

Perhaps the trickiest issue is the careers teacher's dilemma over whether particular pupils should be persuaded that it is in their long-term interests to stay in the sixth form or to take a YTS placement, when the former option will have consequences on the opportunities for other pupils. The administrative difficulties of operating a consortium or links with a college sometimes stretch the resources of the teachers concerned so that they eliminate other tasks which ought to have priority. Careers teachers have often been accused of persuading reluctant pupils to stay at school in order to boost the school's points, while careers officers have been accused of enticing leavers into apprenticeships and trainings! The new schemes do not make this situation any less delicate. Headteachers must be sure that parents understand the range of courses available at sixteen and that college prospectuses are accessible for pupils who may want to visit further education establishments before making final decisions on the next stage, when they are eligible to leave.

Teachers

What sort of person should the headteacher encourage to take up careers work? Is one form of background or one subject-training more useful than another? Should careers teachers have had substantial experience of non-teaching employment, or is that just a desirable extra recommendation? A simpler issue may be the decision to exclude from consideration teachers of vocationally relevant subjects because they may be too heavily associated with a group of occupations to be credible when talking to pupils and parents about the total range of employment. School careers departments need good teachers with diverse strengths, so it may be prudent to keep doors open to any volunteer when there is a vacancy.

The headteacher has to face other issues on staffing the careers department. Can the experience outside teaching of a new member of staff be utilised for its commendable realism in the eyes of pupils? It may be difficult to persuade the head of careers to accept help from someone who just happens to have a light teaching timetable or has time to spare as a result of a rearrangement of pastoral duties. Heads of other departments are not normally expected to take on the induction of someone they would consider unqualified, yet all sorts of teachers are 'offered' to the careers department because they have spare time despite sometimes having no interest or aptitude for the subject.

How does the headteacher reconcile the competing claims of different teachers for the chance of secondment to industry and commerce? It may seem more relevant for teachers of science, business studies or CDT, but the careers teacher has as good a claim as a teacher of mathematics for an introduction to computing or a biologist to health education. Perhaps the easiest way of helping careers teachers is to give them a week during the examination season so that they can be attached to a careers or personnel office. Most of all, they should be encouraged to attend any part-time course on careers education which may be offered by a neighbouring university or college. Other members of staff should appreciate their peculiar circumstances in that teachers seldom have careers in their initial training.

An issue of real difficulty faces any headteacher whose careers teachers are proving ineffective, but who cannot revert to their original specialism. They may be doing real damage to pupils who are expected to suffer ill-prepared classes or ignorant answers to questions on occupations and trainings. Getting rid of unsatisfactory teachers is extremely difficult, but some careers teachers may no longer be energetic enough to cope with a job which requires administrative skills and extra-mural contacts in addition to classroom teaching. The position is more delicate if other departments in the school have established good links with local industry and appear to be more successful in giving pupils insight into the world of work and basic economic understanding.

Equal opportunities

Careers education can be highly influential in widening the horizons and self-concepts of girls, the handicapped and pupils from ethnic minorities. All these youngsters are prone to low aspirations unless appropriately encouraged throughout the formative period of their secondary eduation. It is unfortunate that the choice of subjects for study in the two years before GCSE or 'O' Grades occurs just at the time when girls are becoming aware of their feminine identity and easily influenced by the remarks of boys and what they read in teenage magazines. If they believe that areas of curriculum are somehow more suitable for boys or girls they will choose the stereotypes and avoid what they consider masculine subjects, with a consequent narrowing of their career possibilities. TVEI modules ought to help to combat this, but they need monitoring to achieve the desirable changes in patterns of educational choice. If only it could become the norm in the United Kingdom as it is in the United States and some other countries for boys and girls to stay at school until the age of eighteen and for decisions on subject specialism to be deferred, there might be more genuine equality of career choice.

Can the headteacher inspire all colleagues with the importance of encouraging those pupils most likely to face unemployment? They may be boys and girls from ethnic minorities or non-English speaking homes who know they may have to cope with prejudice when they leave school. Many black girls choose to train as home helps, nursery nurses or hospital catering workers because they believe they will meet less prejudice in those categories, despite their teachers' attempts to assure them that they would be suitable for many other occupations. Positive encouragement to consider a wide range of possibilities applies to both boys and girls if true equality of opportunity is to be achieved. It is especially important that handicapped pupils in mainstream schools should be given positive ideas on what they *can* do rather than the mistaken kindness which has sometimes led to over-emphasis on their disabilities.

LEA policy

Other issues related to the organisation and structure of careers work vary within different LEAs. They include questions of finance, accommodation, resources and teaching time for careers education for students over sixteen who may be assumed to have received sufficient careers education in the main school years. Careers guidance may be affected by the LEA's policy on tertiary colleges, sixth-form centres, consortia and other arrangements for the education of sixteen to nineteen year olds. Particular attention has to be given to those young people living in areas where middle schools separate the guidance on options at thirteen from that on choices at sixteen, or where all post-sixteen education is separated. Extension of the core curriculum or moves towards a nationally prescribed basic curriculum for all will still leave room for choices which will affect later career choices.

The status of the Careers Service within the administrative structure of the authority may be significant. It may be part of the schools branch or of further education or community education, and in some areas it is a separate branch headed by an assistant education officer. The extent of Careers Service involvement in guidance for sixth-formers and college students and its withdrawal from school group work and individual interviews affects the work of careers teachers. Different support is available in areas where there are specially appointed careers officers for older pupils considering higher education and entry to the professions. In most LEAs the Service operates the Advanced Further Education Information service in the summer to give advice to youngsters whose plans for university or college entry may be affected by their 'A' level results. Many eighteen year olds have been guided to an acceptable alternative when their original choices proved unattainable. It supplements the clearing house systems, but only works well if the students have been properly briefed about its function and limitations before they have left school. For many this may be the day of their last examination paper.

The issue of guidance when results come out has been discussed, but may be reinforced by recognition that while schools arrange for examination results to be communicated to pupils there is disquieting evidence of delays in this process and in supplying references for employers. The Careers Service is often the only source of advice for pupils whose plans have been shattered by unexpected failure in a required subject or grade. It would often be preferable for those youngsters to discuss their future with the teacher with whom it was first formulated, but one appreciates that they cannot be required to be available during the holidays. In some schools they do so as volunteers out of concern for the pupils they have nurtured for seven years, but it would be fairer if the LEA could pay them for certain extra attendances at this time in the same way that school teachers are paid to teach in evening institutes. Some headteachers provide careers officers with keys to the pupil records held in the careers room in case of need during the summer holidays.

Policy on the siting of careers resource centres may mean that information on higher and further education or post-graduate careers is kept in a sixth-form block separate from the main school and so inaccessible to younger pupils who may have legitimate need to consult prospectuses or regulations when choosing their subjects.

LEA policy on the in-service training of teachers is especially important for careers because it is a subject almost totally acquired after initial training is completed. Provision within the authority, or funding to enable teachers to attend courses offered by external agencies, is essential. Teachers unfamiliar with the participative and experiential learning methods used in careers classes or with the materials for problem solving, decision taking and self-assessment may be understandably reluctant to take the risk of trying unconventional methods without training. They may also be less successful if pressed to do so by the headteacher, who may need to make a special plea for help in training them.

It may be invidious for the first person to be appointed as an inspector of careers guidance to make a case for more LEAs to appoint such specialists to their team of inspectors and advisers, but careers teachers need the support and help of a careers inspector. It is unrealistic for LEAs to expect the general advisers for secondary education to take more than a cursory interest in the needs of this numerically small, but important, group of teachers. Headteachers can show their belief in the necessity for good careers education by campaigning for the appointment of specialist careers inspectors to advise them on the policies and practices most suitable for their schools. These inspectors can also mount courses of in-service training to increase the confidence needed by careers teachers to face the undoubted difficulty of providing a good programme of careers education and guidance.

Chapter 14
Evaluation and Assessment

Headteachers are increasingly being required to produce a statement of their school's policies on major issues and to undertake some form of evaluation and assessment of the way the schools' aims and objectives are being implemented. For some areas of the curriculum this may be an exercise to quantify examination successes against a formula representing the ability levels of the pupils on entry, with weighting for social and environmental factors. It is not so simple with non-examined subjects such as careers, but it is just as important for teachers to set targets and undertake some self-assessment in order that desirable changes of practice may be considered or extra resources claimed. I do not maintain that what follows represents any clear system, nor that it can be applied universally, but it represents the fruit of long discussion with some highly experienced heads of careers and their senior colleagues.

Resources

It is relatively easy to see whether physical resources are adequate for a proper programme of careers education and guidance. Headteachers have to balance the various priorities between competing claims for each department for space. The careers department needs classrooms, resource centres, an interviewing room, office and library space. It has to compete with others for a share of the clerical assistance available, but its needs must be obvious if a full programme of extra-mural activities is to be established. Record keeping presupposes access to filing systems and methods of communicating information between academic and pastoral colleagues. Even when examination entries and subject options are successfully computerised, some resources will still be necessary to enable teaching colleagues, careers officers or administrative and clerical staff to gain access to extra information. The careers teachers need a share of the back-up available from staff responsible for media resources and reprographic sections.

Teachers' time

It is difficult to assess the validity of careers teachers' claims to be out of school to attend conferences, meetings of local careers associations or to find out more about courses and careers. They do need more non-teaching time than some other colleagues because of the amount of administration required to operate their programme, but the headteacher has to ensure that their release is not at the expense of overburdening others. It they are new to careers work they must have time for training. Fewer schools are likely in future to be able to advertise the post of head of careers to attract external applicants with qualifications or experience in the subject.

Pupils' time

Help in calculating the time needed for pupils at different stages can be obtained from inspectors and principal careers officers. Guidelines have been suggested in Chapter 6. How does a headteacher evaluate the *process* by which young people achieve vocational maturity and can be considered ready to leave school for possible entry to the working world? Is the programme of careers activities such that all pupils can benefit from it or has too much been devoted to the pre-university group or to the problems of the least employable? The quantity of careers work can be measured against a criterion of sufficiency to achieve the aims and objectives of the department, but that takes no account of the process by which the pupils learn. A look at the folders issued as the basis for leavers' survival kits may show whether written work has been properly accomplished and marked as in other subjects. Other non-examination areas of the curriculum may be evaluated by exposure to public criticism and appraisal as in physical education, art, music, drama and crafts, but a programme of careers education cannot easily be assessed by either examinations or displays.

Other criteria

Year to year comparisons measure pupils' activities and the development of talents, skills and knowledge. The careers department can measure its own level of activity by checklists of numbers participating in various parts of its programme, but there is a danger in raising public expectation which a change in the team or provision of resources may render unattainable. The careers teachers should be clearly involved in pupils' subject choices and changing vocational aspirations, and influential in discussions on TVEI modules and new prevocational courses. Some credit may accrue to the careers teachers if, in conjuction with the sixth-form tutors, their advice helps more pupils to obtain preferred places in higher and further education. Headteachers will note with approval the success with which careers teachers follow up leavers and provide material for speech day or annual report to governors from their informal contacts after boys and girls have left. I have sat in careers teachers' offices while twenty year olds knocked on the door to announce success in examinations or promotion in a job – a gratifying recognition of good relationships between teacher and pupils.

Information for incoming parents may take the form of a grid on which the main identifiable occupations are listed and leavers entered in columns according to their level of educational success, so that people can measure an occupational pay-off from schooling. Parents enjoy the reassurance of information on the careers of some previous leavers who were not highly successful in public examinations but later surprised their teachers by getting and keeping worthwhile jobs. Evidence of real concern for the unemployed is equally valuable.

Headteachers expect all heads of department to produce statements of aims and objectives to which their team will work. They must appreciate the difficulty imposed upon heads of careers, however, whose team may be working part of the time in many departments and have pastoral duties specifically connected with careers and thus extra to those undertaken by most teachers. It is particularly important, therefore, for clear aims and objectives to be established for the benefit of those colleagues who may only undertake a little careers work each week or where much is diffused through the pastoral curriculum and subject departments.

The success of a careers department cannot be assessed by the success of leavers in obtaining jobs or training places because this is primarily the task of the careers officers. It may depend more on external factors in the local economy than on leavers' abilities and qualifications. In areas of high unemployment leavers should at least be fully aware of the provisions for the unemployed and knowledgeable about youth centres and classes they might attend.

A possible criterion could be the careers teachers' influence on the extent of pupils' continued education beyond sixteen, but that, too, may depend greatly upon parental attitudes and the local labour market, both of which may persuade many youngsters that staying in education may disadvantage them in getting training or work.

Any evaluation must therefore be to a great extent subjective. The headteacher may look at the process by which pupils attain an agreed measure of vocational maturity or the extent to which they are *employable* as the best assessment of careers teachers' influence upon colleagues teaching those other subjects which develop good communication skills, numeracy, creativity and attitudes to work and the human relationships of the working world. It may be harder to evaluate the success of a careers department than its demonstrable failures. Failure is often a more reliable measure of vocational success than achievement. Those who do well would probably have been equally good at a number of careers, but one can learn much from studying those who fail to settle down in further education or employment. A headteacher hearing that numbers of young people leaving the school have been unable to adjust to the demands of university study or a training course may question whether they chose their courses with or against the advice of their teachers. This may not only reflect the work of careers teachers, but of the school's total teaching style and policy on preparing leavers for adult life and work.

Disagreement between members of staff may arise if some maintain that continued education is always to be preferred by any pupil, while others stake a claim for the advantages of early experience of the responsibilities of the workplace. A policy of careers education for all implies agreement on its importance as a strand running through the curriculum, with varying emphasis and time according to the pupils' progress towards vocational maturity and self-confidence. The team of careers teachers must agree broadly on their aims and objectives and methods of achieving them, while ensuring that these are understood by pastoral and departmental colleagues upon whom they depend for the interchange of information and teaching contributions. Careers education cannot be undertaken in isolation and careers teachers more than many others need to be highly skilled at consultation and collaboration.

Chapter 15
Epilogue

Much discussion has taken place about the impact of new technology and vocational elements in the secondary school curriculum and on the likely employment prospects for young people. Technological innovation in the last thirty years has had dramatic effects upon the jobs available for people at all ages and varying levels of education and qualifications. The question may be asked, 'At what stage should a programme of careers education take this into account?' After all, boys and girls who hope to become doctors, lawyers, chefs or tailors still need the same sort of qualities and training as entrants to those occupations have previously, despite the trend for higher levels of scholastic achievement demanded for many careers. We can forecast a continuing trend in this direction as the requirements of occupations become more rigorous and competition for desirable openings more fierce. Headteachers cannot allow their proper concern for the low-achievers to affect the curriculum in such a way that those who do need traditional qualifications to attain their career aspirations are denied them out of concern for the less fortunate. Academically successful pupils also need the opportunity to develop those other qualities sought by employers which may be most effectively drawn out by experiential learning and out-of-school experiences.

Young people with pronounced talents still require the same chance to develop through art, crafts, music, drama, textiles and pottery as those with scientific and linguistic gifts. All need a curriculum which stretches them appropriately and fits them to pursue courses in higher and further education.

At the same time we are living in a contracting economy in which jobs for the less able are decreasing, while demand is rising for those with the potential to acquire scientific and technological qualifications or train for managerial positions. We cannot foresee how governments will manipulate the economy by legislative or fiscal means, nor the effect this may have on attitudes towards work. It was suggested by Sir George Thomson in *The Foreseeable Future* (1955) that the top quarter of the population in ability, education and drive may have to work a sixty-hour week by the end of this century in order to keep the other three-quarters on social security! Unfortunately, it is those very folk who have most to offer to employment, whether working for an employer, themselves or in a cooperative, who are also most able to make constructive use of time not spent at work. Non-work may be any activity which takes up time and energy without remuneration, as distinct from leisure. The word leisure implies a contrast with time spent economically active 'at work'.

Young people need sympathetic instruction in the economics of wealth creation and labour demand, as well as simple lessons on the cycle of activity by which raw materials become the goods we consume, while other people create wealth by providing services. They must be warned of the rapidity of robotisation to replace machines operated by humans in the post-industrial age. New patterns of working life may await youngsters now at school with periods of full-time education interleaved with spells of work or homemaking and voluntary community service. The retirement age will be lowered, overtime more limited and vacations longer in the more flexible society of the future. Work may be shared in different ways, while people will work at home using new forms of sophisticated office machinery and telecommunications instead of commuting. Those with traditional skills learned in the hard school of apprenticeship and evening study may become disillusioned by the apparent loss of demand for their hard-won skills. This will apply to shorthand-typists as much as metal-working machinists, and draughts-persons as well as cashiers.

The spectre of unemployment has risen dramatically in front of the citizens of most western countries and many futurologists believe we shall never again see the full employment which was for so long an objective of governments. Britain needs a better educated work-force in order to compete internationally because we must continue to produce goods and services for export. Tourism, North Sea oil and international finance cannot on their own keep the economy solvent. Working populations may fluctuate according to the gross domestic product which has been the economists' goal. But there is plenty of work to be done to improve the environment, care for the old, sick, handicapped and those dependent and dejected by reason of prolonged unemployment.

In education there will be new examinations and tests, more use of psychological tests of aptitudes and interests, widespread use of profiling with its risks of subjectivity, but opportunity to highlight achievement and capabilities in an age of increasing demand for talent and credentials.

Careers education must develop too. More sophisticated methods of identifying the requirements of jobs to reduce emphasis upon academic examinations should be matched by better forecasts of the need for workers in different sectors of the economy and at varying levels. This is necessary so that realistic targets can be set before young people while they are still able to choose appropriate education and training programmes.

Planning a youngster's career must be based upon an understanding of the value of flexibility, trainability and the acquisition of transferable skills. At the same time the work ethic which most schools have propagated may no longer be tenable in a future without work for many people. Perhaps schools should think out a policy for careers work based upon a concept of 'life-ethic' by which each person's contribution to society is rated rather than their economic worth expressed in a wage or salary. Each of us has only the ability and talent inherited from our parents, the education which has developed them and the drive to combine the two into a career. Normally this has meant fitting people into specific trainings for the jobs which attracted them, but we can no longer assume that there will be entry to work and a ladder of progress through increasing responsibility and experience recognised by status, power and standard of living.

A person's occupation has been the main means of self-identity and realisation, a symbol of their sense of purpose and contribution to society, exemplified by the life-saving job of a surgeon or ambulance driver, the life-creating function of a mother and home-supporting role of both parents, or by the independent pursuit of a creative urge as artist, writer, musician or architect. It is not necessarily equated with the means of economic survival, although most people would consider occupations to be synonymous with ways of earning a living.

Professor Tom Stonier of Bradford University has suggested that 10 per cent of the workforce will be sufficient by the turn of the century to produce all our material needs for housing, food, clothing, transport and communication. If he is right, how can there be careers for all in the accepted sense? This is not necessarily a situation to be dreaded or deplored because many people were working for forty hours a week for forty years of working life at tasks that were often dull and in some cases dehumanising. Sir Monty Finniston at Imperial College said on 25 October 1979,

The technological revolution which we are now experiencing is of a different order of magnitude and kind from those changes which have preceeded it. The opportunities to relieve man of the burden of work at its worst – dull, repetitive, mindless activities of routine – are a consequence of new technology. The technology of the future is about freeing the individual, not just to control the environment in which he lives but to engage in pursuits more satisfying to himself and others.

A whole-school policy for careers education must be devised to cross subject boundaries and include teachers of all subjects so that boys and girls can develop all their capabilities in order to enable them to live fulfilling lives, if necessary without paid employment. The careers teachers must be instrumental in making things happen, while a greater role is implicit for teachers of moral, political and religious education. Increased resources are also needed for those aesthetic pursuits which for most poeple have little to do with earning a living, but a great deal to do with the enrichment of life. At the same time, teachers should show pupils the exciting opportunities which an education based upon specialisation in mathematics and physical science can provide.

Pupils need help in developing their capability to design and make things, to perform as well as analyse and dissect. They need more opportunity for communication, decision taking, problem solving and the exercise of judgement on perceived facts and evidence if they are to be more innovative and to formulate a personal system of values by which to live.

The low proportion of young people remaining voluntarily in education beyond the statutory leaving age is a blot on the British education system when compared with many comparable countries. Perhaps the tragedy of high unemployment, with its particular effect upon school-leavers, may be a sufficient spur to render acceptable to a greater number of youngsters the idea of continued education at sixteen or later. The opportunity to develop skills for employability will still be needed because young people must occupy their time and may find even more important in future those life and social skills which are necessary for survival in a complex society.

Careers education has an integrating function in schools to help pupils see possible future roles and appreciate why so much is changing around them. It should also encourage them with a sense of their own worthwhileness as people, even if they are not going to earn a wage as evidence of adult status. Careers classes should be seminal in spreading the seeds of self-confidence and hope for the future. It must influence those youngsters with the potential to be the managers, professionals, creators and teachers of the future. Teachers have a responsibility to be sure they do not fail the next generation by discouraging those able pupils on whom the future depends. A technological society may not need so many workers, but its influence and extension cannot be stayed. Teachers must recognise this if there is to be the hoped-for rising standard of living for all and better care for the disadvantaged in our society. In the apt words of the Crowther Report *15 to 18* in 1960:

> There is a duty to reconsider those other objectives of any education which have little or nothing to do with vocation, but are concerned with the development of human personality and with teaching the individual to see himself in due proportion to the world in which he has been set . . . Children are not the 'supply' that meets any 'demand', however urgent. They are individual human beings and the primary concern of the schools should not be with the living they will earn but with the life they will lead.

Topics for staff discussion

1. Strategies should be planned to cope with the essential curriculum and to make provision for careers work. In a situation of falling rolls teachers must ensure fair consideration of the needs of the most and least academically able. Which subjects can be taught on a wholly mixed-ability basis for what age groups?
2. If the careers teachers list the constraints imposed upon their work by the organisation, staffing or premises of the school, staff discussion may be able to eliminate some.
3. Experienced teachers can produce examples of constraints imposed upon individual pupils' future courses and careers by the examination policy of the school and elicit suggestions from colleagues of the appropriate action to minimise damage to those pupils' prospects in similar situations.
4. Taking any of the issues in Chapter 13 which seem to the headteacher to be important or topical, a member of staff may be persuaded to introduce discussion designed to promote greater awareness or propose action.
5. A staff meeting can formulate a brief document outlining to parents and employers the school's policy and practice on careers work.
6. 'Work is what you do for yourself or for society, whether it is paid for or not,' said Professor Wrenn at Keele University. Do all teachers accept this definition and express it in their relations with pupils and the school community?
7. How can those staff who believe in the importance of careers education defend its place in the life of the school against non-believers?
8. All members of staff with useful contacts outside in higher and further education, employment and voluntary agencies can contribute to the work of careers teachers and officers. How can this be maximised for pupils' benefit and individuals be persuaded to relinquish some of their private contacts for greater efficiency and fairness overall?
9. Secondary-school teachers have sometimes accused local colleges of 'body-snatching'; would a joint in-service training course increase cooperation and reduce rivalry?
10. Can a staff meeting establish priorities for the secondment of teachers to industry and commerce or to various courses?
11. Members of staff in other departments may be able to help the head

of careers with suggestions and contributions to the in-service training of new careers teachers.

12. While equal opportunities in education and careers may be endorsed in principle by all members of staff some may be unwilling to accept its consequences for their own work; what form of in-service training is most appropriate for its realisation?

13. How does a proposed or imposed change of structure from an eleven to eighteen school to some form of break between those ages affect the careers work and opportunities for pupils?

14. How much careers education should be included in a national core curriculum?

15. To what use can the period during and after summer examinations be put to promote in-service training of teachers?

16. If financial compensation were available, which teachers would be willing to take part in arrangements to help pupils during the holiday period immediately after examination results are published? Do staff generally regard this as necessary/desirable/equitable?

17. What new activities, methods and content do teachers feel call for in-service training and how can it be provided?

18. Assuming a general requirement to keep departments of the school under review, how does the head of careers tackle the task and can a checklist of factors be drawn up at a staff meeting for assessing the school's total effort in preparing leavers for adult and working life?

19. Some people maintain that young people have the right to choose not to work while others reject the notion of a class of young adults living off the labour of others. If these attitudes are reflected in the staffroom, how do they affect INSET proposals?

20. I once heard the late Herman Kahn, Director of the Hudson Institute, say at a conference of American school counsellors: 'The world is too good a place to be without faith in the future'. This would make a suitable text for a school in-service training day on the purpose of preparing pupils for adult and working life and the justification for careers across the curriculum.

Bibliography

Avent, C., *Practical Approaches to Careers Education* (CRAC/Hobsons, 1974, 4th ed. 1985).
Ball, B., *Careers Counselling in Practice* (Falmer, 1984).
Bazalgette, J., *School Life and Work Life* (Hutchinson, 1978).
Best, R., Jarvis, C., and Ribbins, P., *Perspectives on Pastoral Care* (Heinemann, 1980).
British Institute of Management, *Industry, Education and Management* (BIM, 1979).
Cleaton, D.R, and Foster, R.J., *Practical Aspects of Guidance* (Careers Consultants, 1982).
Cleaton, D.R., *Survey of Careers Work* (Newpoint, 1987).
Cooper, N., *School Industry Link Schemes* (DES, 1981).
Department of Education and Science, *15 to 18* (HMSO, 1960).
DES, *Careers Education in Secondary Schools* (HMSO, 1973).
DES, *Curriculum 11–16* (HMSO, 1977).
DES, *Aspects of Secondary Education in England* (HMSO, 1979).
DES, *School Examinations* (HMSO, 1978).
DES, *A Framework For the School Curriculum* (HMSO, 1980).
DES, *A View of the Curriculum* (HMSO, 1980).
DES, *Records of Achievement* (HMSO, 1984).
DES, *Education For All* (HMSO, 1985).
DES/Department of Employment, *Working Together For a Better Future* (COI, 1987).
Department of Industry, *Engineering Our Future* (HMSO, 1980).
Further Education Curriculum Review and Development Unit (FEU) *A Basis For Choice* (HMSO, 1979).
FEU, *Basic Skills* (DES, 1982).
FEU, *CPVE in action* (DES, 1985).
FEU, *Developing Social and Life Skills* (HMSO, 1980).
Hill, J.M.M. and Scharff, D.E., *Between Two Worlds* (Careers Consultants, 1976).
Jackson, R. (ed.), *Careers Guidance: Practice and Problems* (Arnold, 1973).
Jamieson, A., and Lightfoot, M., *Schools and Industry* (Methuen, 1982).
Jamieson, I., *Industry in Education* (Longman, 1985).
Law, B. and Watts, A.G., *Schools, Careers and Community* (Church Information Office, 1977).
Law, B., *The Pre-Vocational Franchise* (Harper and Row, 1987).
Marland, M., *The Experience of Work* (Longman, 1973).
Marland, M., *Pastoral Care* (Heinemann, 1974).

Maclure, S., *Education and Youth Employment in Great Britain* (Carnegie Council on Policy Studies in Higher Education, 1979).

Oxford Review of Education, Vol. 44 No. 3 (OUP, 1978).

Pratt, J., Bloomfield, J., and Searle, C., *Option Choice* (NFER/Nelson, 1984).

Pring, R., *Personal and Social Education in the Curriculum* (Hodder and Stoughton, 1984).

Rogers, B., *Careers Education and Guidance*, (CRAC/Hobsons, 1984).

Schools Council, Enquiry No. 1. *Young School Leavers* (HMSO, 1968).

Schools Council, Working Paper 40, *Careers Education in the Seventies* (Evans/Methuen, 1972).

Stonier, T., *The Wealth of Information* (Methuen, 1983).

Thompson, R. and Walford, G., *Teachers Into Industry* (Aston Education Monograph 11, 1983).

Thomson, G., *The Foreseeable Future* (Cambridge University Press, 1955).

Wallace, R.G., *Introducing Technical and Vocational Education* (Macmillan, 1985).

Watts, A.G., Super, D.E. and Kidd, J.M., *Career Development in Britain* (CRAC/Hobsons, 1981).

Watts, A.G., *Education, Unemployment and the Future of Work* (Open University Press, 1983).

Watts, A.G., *Work Experience and Schools* (Heinemann, 1983).

Appendix: Useful Addresses for School–Industry Links

CRAC Insight Programme, Sheraton House, Castle Park, Cambridge, CB3 OAX

Grubb Institute of Behaviourial Studies, The EWR Centre, Cloudesley Street, London, N1 OHV

INDEX, 91 Waterloo Road, London, SE1 8XP

Industrial Society Challenge of Industry, etc., Robert Hyde House, 48 Bryanston Square, London, W1H 7LN

Schools Curriculum Industry Partnership, Newcombe House, 45 Notting Hill Gate, London, W11 3JB

Trident Trust, Robert Hyde House, 48 Bryanston Square, London, W1H 7LN

TVEI Unit, Manpower Services Commission, 236 Grays Inn Road, London, WC1X 8HL

Understanding British Industry, Sun Alliance House, New Inn Hall Street, Oxford, OX1 2QE

Understanding Industry, 91 Waterloo Road, London, SE1 8XP

Young Enterprise, Robert Hyde House, 48 Bryanston Square, London, W1H 7LN

Index